LOSING OUT

Books by Frank Field

As author
Unequal Britain (1974)
Inequality In Britain: Freedom, Welfare And The State (1981)
Poverty And Politics (1982)
The Minimum Wage: Its Potential And Dangers (1984)
Freedom And Wealth In A Socialist Future (1987)
The Politics Of Paradise (1987)

As co-author
To Him Who Hath: A Study Of Poverty And Taxation (1976)

As editor
20th Century State Education (jointly) (1971)
Black Britons (jointly) (1971)
Low Pay (1973)
Are Low Wages Inevitable? (1976)
Education And The Urban Crisis (1976)
The Conscript Army: A Study Of Britain's Unemployed (1976)
The Wealth Report 1 (1979)
The Wealth Report 2 (1983)
Politices Against Low Pay: An International Perspective (1984)

FRANK FIELD

LOSING OUT

The Emergence of Britain's Underclass

Basil Blackwell

Copyright © Frank Field 1989

First published 1989

Basil Blackwell Ltd
108 Cowley Road, Oxford, OX4 1JF, UK

Basil Blackwell Inc.
3 Cambridge Center,
Cambridge, MA 02142, USA

British Library Cataloguing in Publication Data
A CIP catalogue record for this book is available
from the British Library

Library of Congress Cataloging in Publication Data
Field, Frank, 1942–
Losing Out: The Emergence of Britain's Underclass / Frank Field.
   p.   cm.
Includes index.
ISBN 0–631–17148–7
ISBN 0–631–17149–5 (pbk.)
1. Poor—Great Britain. 2. Economic assistance, Domestic—Great Britain.   I. Title.
HC260. P6P573   1989
362.5'0941—dc20   89–32979
                                                          CIP

Typeset in 10 on 12 pt Ehrhardt
by Wearside Tradespools, Fulwell, Sunderland
Printed in Great Britain by Billing and Sons Ltd., Worcester

Contents

For Ruth Runciman

Preface

John Lloyd was the first person to suggest that I should write a book on the emergence of an underclass in Britain. In following his suggestion a large number of people have helped me. Damian Leeson, Thomas Meyer, Ben Plowden and Joan Hammell worked in preparing the manuscript for the press. Carole Andrews, Christopher Barclay, Jeremy Brevitt, Philippa Carling, Rob Clements, Richard Cracknell, Adrian Crompton, Dora Clark, Timothy Edmonds, Eric Fishwick, Oonagh Gay, Christine Gillie, Julia Lourie, Betty McInnes, Brenda Mee, Keith Parry, David Plowright, Robert Twigger and Barry Winetrobe of the House of Commons Library either traced publications for me or undertook calculations used in *Losing Out*. Nick Allen copy-edited the book. I would also like to thank Seán Magee, my editor at Blackwell, and Andrew McNeillie for their support in bringing the book to press. While I am grateful to each person for their help, I alone remain responsible for the presentation of the argument.

Birkenhead   February 1989

Introduction

Citizenship and Social Class

Alfred Marshall, in a paper read to the Cambridge Reform Club in 1873, on 'The future of the working classes', posed the dilemma: 'whether there be valid ground for the opinion that the amelioration of the working classes has limits beyond which it cannot pass' (quoted in T. H. Marshall, *Citizenship and Social Class*, Cambridge University Press, 1950, p. 4). The issue was not, Marshall commented, 'whether all men will ultimately be equal – that they certainly will not – but whether progress may not go on, readily, if slowly, till, by occupation at least, every man is a gentleman.' Marshall, in answer to his own question, concluded 'I hold that it may and that it will.'

Marshall's optimism stemmed from what he observed to be happening to the skilled artisans during the heyday of Victorian capitalism. T. H. Marshall drew on these passages in his 1949 lecture, 'Citizenship and social class', in order to set the progressive movement within a much grander historical perspective. According to T. H. Marshall, one of the characteristics of British history over the past three centuries has been an extension of what we would now call the different aspects of citizenship, with civil rights, or citizenship, being largely established in the eighteenth century, political citizenship in the nineteenth, and social and economic citizenship constituting the agenda for the current century.

While a careful study reveals that each phase in the build-up of Britain's modern political community does not fit neatly into these century-long categories – the universal franchise was only fully established this century, for example, and plural voting was abolished only a year before Marshall gave his lecture – this approach none the less provides a sense of an incorporating movement that has resulted in what is today recognizable as the basis of modern citizenship. This movement towards guaranteeing a universal citizenship, however, was one compatible with the continuing existence of social class differences. Indeed, T. H. Marshall posed the question: 'is it still true that basic equality, when enriched in substance and embodied in the formal rights of citizenship, is consistent with the inequalities of social class?' Marshall, who like his mentor Alfred delighted in answering his own questions, replied: 'our society today assumes that the two are still compatible.'

The main thrust of *Losing Out* is that the 300-year evolution of citizenship as an incorporating force in British society has been thrown into reverse. Or, to use Alfred Marshall's terminology, not every man or woman will now become a gentleman or gentlewoman. It will be argued here that four forces have brought about this reversal: the record post-war levels of unemployment; widening class differences; exclusion of the very poorest from rapidly rising living standards; and a significant change in public attitudes towards those people who are seen to have failed to 'make it' in Mrs Thatcher's Britain. These four forces have operated in the ways outlined below, and have combined to produce an underclass that sits uncomfortably below that group which is referred to as living on a low income.

Causes of the Underclass

First, the effect of unemployment is considered. The brief period of full employment following World War Two provided, for the first time, a universal escape from a Poor Law culture, where poverty, personal failure and shame were inextricably interwoven. Full employment provided an income independent of welfare for all those who wished to work and, as will be seen below, ensured a greater degree of equality in income distribution than has been effected at any other time. Being in work automatically led to workers accruing for themselves, and to some extent their families, rights to social insurance benefits, and, latterly, acted as the gateway to a range of company welfare. In contrast, unemployment has not only countered these trends, but has also had a crucial effect on the direction of social mobility. Studies since the 1930s have shown a rapid social rise for a significant proportion of children born to working-class parents. This trend continues, but is now accompanied by a downward mobility for those denied access to the labour market.

Second, the scope of class divisions. The dominant characteristic of British society has been its polarization along class lines, although this tendency was countered by a bipartisan political approach aimed at preventing a deterioration in class differences (see Peter Jenkins, *Mrs Thatcher's Revolution*, Jonathan Cape, 1987, which questions how long into the post-war period this bipartisanship lasted). This is also no longer so. It has been the deliberate aim of the Thatcher Governments to reshape British culture around an enterprise ethos, and, for the first time ever, the official statistics show class divisions widening along a broad front. While unemployment has had an immediate and brutally limiting effect on the idea of a universal citizenship, widening class differences have begun to have a similar, if more subtle effect in breaking up the sense of common citizenship, whereby each of us feels we belong to the same society.

Third, excluding the poor from rapidly rising living standards. In the late 1950s the Conservative Government decided that those on the lowest incomes should share in the increase in national income apparent at the time. This policy has now been vetoed, even though living standards are rising at a record rate. Instead of keeping the living standards of this group in line with rises enjoyed by other groups in the population, the present Government has reverted to the much more limited approach of only protecting benefit levels from rising prices. Such a policy has, of course, affected the relative living standards of all claimants dependent on income support – driving an ever wider wedge between them and all other groups in the community – but has most adversely affected those people who are dependent on this form of welfare for long periods of time.

Fourth, a significant change in public attitudes. This has led to a psychological and political separation of the very poorest from the rest of the community. There are obvious dangers arising from trying to plot shifts in public attitudes, especially as one of the peculiarities of the English is to overestimate the more positive aspects of the immediate past. Siegfried Sassoon, writing in the trenches in World War One, caught this characteristic in his remark that for the British, promotion from Inferno to Paradise would be accompanied by a harking back to the good old days. However, despite the danger of sentimentalizing the past, there does appear to be a weight of evidence in favour of the importance solidarity played in working-class life. That value is much less evident today, and has to a significant degree been replaced by a 'drawbridge' mentality. That is, those from working-class backgrounds who have done well have been keen to ensure that their former peers do not benefit in the same degree as themselves. Instead of wishing to see others advance, this group has been anxious to raise the drawbridge behind them once their own upward social mobility has taken place. This trend has been reflected in the political arena, with the Labour Party finding it harder than ever to build a coalition of voters with common interests.

Large numbers of people currently find their status as citizens under attack from one or more of these expelling forces. Some citizens find themselves experiencing the force of all four agents simultaneously, and to such an extent that they are being relegated into what is described here as an underclass. They increasingly live under what is a subtle form of political, social and economic apartheid. Indeed, the emergence of an underclass marks a watershed in Britain's class politics. Today, the very poorest are separated, not only from other groups on low incomes, but, more importantly, from the working class. This latter group shares with other social classes the hope of ever-rising living standards and opportunities. These shared aspirations now appear as a more powerful uniting agent than the personal and political differences arising from the massive disparities in income and wealth in this newly formed coalition.

Membership of the Underclass

Losing Out sees this underclass as being recruited from three groups. First, the recruiting sergeant has been active in the ranks of the long-term unemployed. It is wrong, however, to think of the unemployed as a homogeneous group, equally prey to enrolment into the ranks of the underclass. Even at the peak period of post-war unemployment – January 1986 – 233,000 unemployed people were leaving the register each month. Unemployment continued to rise because 379,000 people registered as unemployed during the same period. Amongst this ebb and flow on and off the register are two groups who have been without work for a long period, and it is these groups that are most prone to membership of the underclass. These are those school leavers who have never had a job, and those older workers who have been without work for very long periods.

A second distinct group of claimants with little hope of freeing themselves from dependence on welfare are single-parent families. Had there not been a massive increase in unemployment since 1979, much of the public debate would currently be focused on the more than 200 per cent increase in the numbers of single mothers on welfare in the last eight years. This category of welfare claimants similarly should not be seen as a homogeneous group. As with the unemployed, there are a considerable number of single mothers who draw benefit for only a short period of time; they are fortunate in being able to take one or more of the escape routes from dependency. (What these are, and how such opportunities can be multiplied is considered in Part IV.) What is of maximum concern is that group of single mothers dependent on welfare for very long periods of time.

The third group of very poor claimants, for whom there is no prospect for improvement if current policies continue, are elderly pensioners. This group is totally dependent on their old-age pension and income support. None of them has any occupational pension; many of them live in the worst housing conditions, and their income does not adequately compensate for the extra expense arising from the disabilities that accompany extreme old age.

Despite the provisos already expressed, identification of these three groups is too crude a measurement of the underclass. How long-term unemployment affects a person's attitudes and well-being varies not only according to the individual's psychological make-up, but also that person's interaction with the surrounding environment. Again, generalizations are dangerous, but unemployment can have less of a psychological effect on someone who is laid off in an area of high employment than in an area where unemployment is less common. Yet even here a distinction needs to be drawn between the person whose family is in work, and can be financially supportive, and one whose unemployment is the common experience, not only of the unemployed person's family, but for many of their friends as well. Then there are those unemployed people who, despite all the odds, manage to prevent themselves slipping into despondency. Similarly, being a single-parent family has a different effect if a person's qualifications or experience are those in high demand by potential employers, and the extended family is well placed on the income scale, rather than being on welfare themselves. Again a distinction needs to be drawn between those elderly pensioners living on income support who are looked after by family and friends, and those who lack any additional financial resources, and who are without support from either family or neighbours.

A Counter View

In an early contribution to the debate on the underclass in this country, Ralf Dahrendorf, one of the most perceptive and gifted observers on the British scene, also argues that the advent of mass unemployment has been the catalyst bringing the underclass into existence ('The erosion of citizenship and its consequences for us all', *New Statesman*, 12 June 1987). Expressed in basic terms, the issue arises because the capital base in advanced Western economies is now so extensive that a 'shrinking labour force of increasing skill will produce more'. Dahrendorf believes that, with respect to industrial development, the West may now have reached a point similar to that long since passed in agriculture, where mountains of goods can be produced with significantly reduced numbers of producers.

If the underclass is a product of underemployment and unemployment, Dahrendorf sees a further distinguishing characteristic of this new class in terms of social pathologies:

Members of the underclass tend to have a low level of educational attainment; many have not finished school; there is much functional and absolute illiteracy. Incomplete families are the rule rather than the exception. Housing conditions for the underclass are usually miserable; to some extent, this class is an inner-city phenomenon.   (p. 13)

Dahrendorf believes that the underclass is beginning to form its own culture.

It includes a lifestyle of laid-back sloppiness, association in changing groups or gangs, congregation around discos or the like, hostility to middle-class society, particular habits of dress, hairstyle, often drugs or at least alcohol – a style, in other words which has little in common with the values of the work society around.   (p. 13)

Any description of the underclass is bound to highlight the social and cultural characteristics of the group. Yet there is a danger of these characteristics being interpreted as the 'causes' of the problem itself, and from this it is only a short step to falling into the syndrome of 'blaming the victim'.

Discussion regarding the root causes of the underclass can, similarly, all too easily become prey to an exclusively 'culture of poverty' approach. To put it more crudely, but no less accurately, this approach suggests that the poor continue to breed amongst themselves attitudes and values which are the seeds of their continuing destruction. This is the tenor of Nicholas Lemann's influential contribution to the American debate ('The origins of the underclass', *Atlantic Monthly*, June 1986). In the US, the underclass is seen largely as a racial phenomenon, and Lemann writes that:

[the] underclass did not just spring into being over the past 20 years. Every aspect of the underclass culture in the ghettos is directly traceable to roots in the South – not the South of slavery, but the South of a generation ago. In fact, there seems to be a strong correlation between the underclass status in the North, and a family background in the nascent underclass of the sharecropper South. (p. 35)

It would be wrong to dismiss out of hand this 'culture of poverty' interpretation, given that the attributes of the poor do need to be considered, and indeed are so explored in the final section. But by considering this approach in isolation we run the risk of shifting the search for counter-policies into a backwater of measures dealing only with the distinguishing characteristics displayed by some members of the underclass.

A concentration on what are perceived as moral weaknesses exhibited by the underclass is hardly novel. My own local newspaper, the *Birkenhead News*, regularly carried stories throughout the inter-war years about the town being populated by those who had ceased wanting to work. When war came in 1939, the shipyard's order-book was boosted to overflowing, and the town walked quietly back to work. Fifty years later, it would hardly be surprising, after what are often hundreds of failed job applications, if some of the unemployed did not reject those values most associated with the work ethic.

And yet, stated objections to some of society's values should not blind the rest of society to the underclass's commitment to the cornerstone value of the whole system – work itself. What evidence there is suggests that most young people are anxious to work. A survey in three contrasting areas of the North-East concluded that while 'a clear majority were non-political, pragmatic young adults', they 'were also eager for employment, even on modest wages' (*ESRC Newsletter*, no. 61, November 1987, p. 17). This group, 'far from advancing a rebellious morality, were conservative on most social issues, and . . . had turned their frustrations not against their elders, but against themselves'. Such conservatism was not based on any false expectation about their own immediate employment prospects, which they described as 'shit jobs, govvy schemes, or the dole'. Significantly, the survey failed to support a social pathology explanation of the underclass's existence.

Losing Out does not maintain that full employment is going to be gained as easily as it was with the coming of World War Two and the massive expansion of central government expenditure on armaments. It does, however, take issue with those – invariably in work themselves – who argue that full employment is a thing of the past. Changes may well need to be made in the length of the working week, and the increase in wages sought by those in work, in return for a more expedient trade-off of job opportunities for those without work. But the significance of this commitment to full employment must not be underrated.

The personal pathologies of many of the underclass, and the culture induced by poverty, need to be seen as part, but only part, of a score of social and economic maladies against which action needs to be taken. Above all, it is vital to get away from the notion that the part of the underclass of working age is in some way responsible for their own exclusion from the mainstream of society. Such an exclusion undoubtedly exists, and is indeed one of the key characteristics of this group, but members of the group are equally characterized by a wish to regain membership – through a job – as soon as possible. *Losing Out* maintains that without a return to full employment, there will be no effective counter to the condition of the underclass.

Censoring Information

Trying to plot a new social development is a hazardous undertaking at the best of times. It is particularly so at present, owing to two quite distinct causes. The first is the Government's censoring of sensitive data on class differences, which are vital to the identification of changes in people's life chances.

Over the past 150 years, British governments have built up an impressive array of statistical information, and much of it has been used by social researchers to describe, with varying degrees of success, the society in which they have lived. Since 1979, however, the Government has begun to censor a whole range of statistical information previously available to the public, and this reduction is particularly noticeable in the sensitive areas that detail the changing degree of inequality in Britain. Here some of the main moves by the Government on this front are noted. (Other equally important acts of censorship are detailed in Part I.)

The Wilson Government established a standing Royal Commission that reported regularly on the changing distribution of income and wealth. The Commission reworked existing series of data on income and wealth, as well as regularly commissioning special surveys. Soon after winning the 1979 election, Mrs Thatcher announced the Commission's abolition. The scope of the General Household Survey, which commenced in 1971, and which could best be described as a 'state of Britain' report, has been considerably curtailed. The Supplementary Benefits Commission, which acted as an official watchdog over the interests of those people on benefit, and which regularly published an overall view of the circumstances of those on low incomes, was quietly, but efficiently dispatched in 1980.

Since 1979, the Government has instituted more than twenty changes in the presentation of the unemployment data which have resulted in a statistical fall in the numbers of unemployed. In some of the publications that have remained in existence, the Government has blocked the inclusion of sensitive information. The table providing the link between unemployment and ill health, for example, no longer appears in the current issue of *Social Trends*.

It is difficult to conduct a public debate if part of the Government's energies are used to suppress the material vital in making that debate effective. But there are other examples of the ways in which the Government has attempted to stem the flow of information bearing directly on the emergence of an underclass in Britain. During the 1960s, the Wilson Government doubled the size of the Family Expenditure Survey (FES), in order that studies of minority groups, such as the poor and blacks, could be carried out on a regular basis. In fact, the only analyses to have been carried out were on the numbers and composition of low-income groups. This information was published on an annual basis up until the 1979 election, after which the

Thatcher Government announced that such information would only be released every other year.

The Government's defence was that such a move would contribute to cutting public expenditure. The 1985 Low Income Families data were not published until 1988, when the Government declared that it would cease publication of this series altogether. In its place, it has begun to release information on the relative living standards of people in the lowest decile income groups. If the Government has its way, no comprehensive information will be available on the numbers on low income, and how these have changed over time, either with respect to fiscal and welfare reforms, or, just as importantly, the rate of economic growth.

Another example of the Government blocking the publication of information centres on the mortality data (see p. 58 on the way in which the Government attempted to block publication of the Black Report). Every ten years, the Registrar General publishes an analysis of death by occupation, cause of death, sex and age as a supplement to the National Census. The supplement analysing the data from the Census of 1970–2 was almost twice as long as the supplement published in 1986 and included around sixty pages that considered social class differences in mortality. In stark contrast the most recent report contains only 128 pages of commentary, of which only five pages are concerned with an analysis of death according to social class. While the report is published with eighty-seven microfiches of tables, which does represent an increase in the amount of 'publicly available information', access to them is obviously restricted, not only by the price of the report and each set of microfiche (£49.20), but by the need for access to a microfiche reader and the skill needed in order to analyse the data presented in the tables.

Mrs Thatcher's Role

The whole process of making it more difficult for commentators to gain a clear conception of the emergence and dimensions of the underclass has been reinforced by the inability of many to appreciate the economic changes that the Thatcher Governments have brought about, even though there is now a considerable amount of publicly available information on this score. More importantly, a significant part of the left seems incapable of appreciating the nature and dimension of recent economic developments. This stance is buttressed by the unspoken assumption that Thatcherism is an aberration from a historical norm, and that, in the post-Thatcher era, the old values and means of attending to political questions will once again reassert themselves. Such a belief could not be further from the truth.

Ironically, however, it has been the Prime Minister herself who has been most at pains to stress the extent to which 1979 marked the breaking of the existing political mould. The truth is rather different. Although the Governments elected since 1979 have made a marked breach with the consensus politics of the 1950s and 1960s, Mrs Thatcher's approach and views fit easily into the mould made by Bonar Law, Baldwin and Chamberlain. Stuart Ball, in his study of the Conservative Party between 1929 and 1931, comments:

The mass of the Conservative Party, in the constituencies and on the backbenches, are not intellectuals. They have not been converted since 1975 to an economic ideology for which 'monetarism' or 'Thatcherism' are abbreviations... On the contrary, the reason for the appeal of that policy is that it is, under cover of much economic jargon, the traditional, indeed the instinctive, Conservative remedy in times of recession. (*Baldwin and the Conservative Party*, Yale University Press, 1988, p. 218)

If Thatcherism is not, then, a new form of British Conservatism, but a return to the norm, then those who wish to regain a society characterized by full employment – and the values that stem from it – can see just how large the task is. The belief of some commentators that full employment has been a constant feature of British economic life this century, from which the 1970s and 1980s are a temporary and easily reversible deviation, is clearly false. It is in their having been characterized by full employment, as much as anything else, that the exceptional quality of the two post-war decades lies.

There is, however, a paradox here. Mrs Thatcher's return to the norm, under the cloak of making a radical departure from it, should not disguise the success that she has had since 1979, particularly in the economic sphere. It is here that a second factor that obscures what is occurring comes into play. I am concerned here specifically with the detestation with which the left regards Mrs Thatcher, an abhorrence so profound that it is unable to view dispassionately the Government's record.

The left's response is, of course, crucial, for it is from this quarter alone that policies to counter the status of an underclass can emerge. However, the signs on this front are not promising, primarily because, in denying the economic successes that have occurred since 1981, the left is unable to appreciate that it is not the lack of economic growth, but its distribution that is a fundamental cause of the underclass's existence. To be aware of the significance of the economic changes that have occurred in British society since 1979 is not the same as stating agreement with everything the Prime Minister has done. But no analysis of where Britain is now, and is likely to be in the next century, can afford to ignore the economic counter-revolution through which we have lived and, particularly, the recent growth in the economy.

The Importance of Economic Growth

Historically, Britain's rate of economic growth has been low compared with that of most Western European countries. During the inter-war years, the overall rate averaged 1.2 per cent per year. Even during the immediate post-war years, which were concerned with rebuilding a war-stricken economy, the annual rate of growth averaged only 1.4 per cent. Despite the boom of the 1950s and the early 1960s, the economy was dogged by a series of balance of payments crises. Over most of this period, the Government, instead of attempting to increase the under-lying level of investment, manipulated the economy largely by determining the level of consumer expenditure. Increases on this front initially resulted in a period of rapid economic growth that was quickly brought to a standstill as a result of a structural weakness in the British economy. The increases in consumer demand were not met from the home market, but largely by imports. The result was an increase in the balance of payments deficit, and a curtailment of the consumer boom by the Government's focus on interest rates. This period of the post-war economy was characterized by what became known as the 'stop–go' approach.

In 1979, it looked as though the stop–go cycle was set to continue; the following two years were marked by a clearly defined stop. Unemployment rose rapidly, and, despite Government manipulation of the figures, reached a record post-war level of 3.25 million in mid-1986. Since then there has been a period of sustained economic growth. The average annual growth rate since 1981 has been 3.1 per cent – nearly treble the inter-war rate, and considerably more than twice the rate of economic growth of the post-war years. (For how this compares internationally, see Martin Woolf, 'Is there a British miracle?', *Financial Times*, 16 June, 1988.)

The Labour Party seems incapable of understanding the significance of these economic changes. Its response has largely been to prophesy imminent collapse, not just of the boom, but, on some occasions, of the economy itself. Certainly, the balance on manufacturing trade is disturbing, with the current imbalance heading towards record levels. With the oil revenues beginning to decline significantly, or so the argument runs, this deficit is not only unsustainable, but is likely to force the economy into reverse.

Clearly, an economy that has traditionally grown at an average level of below 1.5 per cent will be unable to sustain the 7 per cent growth rate recorded for part of 1988. However, the difficulties involved in achieving a soft landing for the British economy should not be underestimated. particularly if the Government is prepared to use interest rates as the only measure to bring inflation under control. Moreover, while part of the deficit on manufacturing trade is accounted for by the volume of capital goods imported, this has not been as significant a cause of the deteriorating trade balance as the Government has tried to claim. Investing in appropriate capital goods is crucial if a high level of economic growth is to be maintained. It is equally important that the productivity gains that have been made over the past six years are sustained, although again the difficulties involved should not be underestimated. Marking up impressive gains on this front is much easier following an economy's move out of recession than it is when the economy has been growing at a record level for some time.

One further factor has escaped the notice of most commentators. While the cushioning effect of North Sea oil is now less than it was, the increase in dividends being returned to this country as a result of overseas investments, particularly those made over the past decade, is beginning to play an increasingly important part in the balance of payments. In 1980, earnings on overseas investments were about equal to the sum earned by the dividends on UK investments held by overseas residents, £5,799 and £5,857 million respectively. By 1987, this position had changed markedly, with £16,567 million being earned on overseas investments, compared with £9,135 million earned for foreigners on their investments in this country (see Central Statistical Office database series, HHBY, CGNV, HHCH, HERN).

For all these reasons, the British economy is therefore more soundly based than Labour has so far cared to admit. Prophesying the imminent collapse of the British economy has diverted attention from those fundamental changes in the constituent parts of the economy that are having a long-term political impact.

A No-shares Approach

The most significant change for the purpose of this essay is not so much the unequal way these gains of economic growth have been shared between different groups of the population, important though this is, but rather that a minority have been excluded from benefiting at all. Growth, far from having the unifying influence it has had in the past, is now being used to separate a significant group of the population from their fellow citizens. This economic separation is being reinforced by a fundamental political development.

The means by which the Government has effected this distribution has been through unemployment as well as through a whole range of tax and fiscal changes. Unemployment has had a dual effect on the distribution of income: those excluded from work invariably suffer a large drop in personal income; exclusion of a large group from the labour market also affects the overall distribution of income, making it far more unequal.

The Government's tax and welfare strategies have also had a dual impact on Britain's social stratification. Its aim has been not merely to polarize society still further, but also, in the case of some of the welfare changes, introduce an element of expulsion from what had hitherto been thought of as a person's social insurance rights. The tax cuts since 1979 have overwhelmingly been of benefit to those on high incomes, and the higher the income the greater the tax cuts have been. The richest 1 per cent of taxpayers in 1988–9 alone gained tax cuts worth £4.2 billion. In order to pay for these tax cuts, the Government has implemented a sustained attack on the level of welfare payments. In the current year, on a conservative estimate, savings on the welfare budget have been around £5 billion – a sum that has paid for the tax cuts to the richest 1 per cent of income earners, and leaves a little small change for other high-income groups. The welfare savings have been made by employing a number of related strategies. First, the benefit paid to the unemployed has been either cut or abolished. On no less than seventeen occasions since 1979 the Government has brought in changes eroding the right to employment benefit (see A. B. Atkinson and J. Micklewright, *Turning the Screw*, STICERD, LSE, London, 1988). In addition, twenty-one other welfare changes have been introduced – the vast majority having an adverse effect on the income of the unemployed.

Until 1987, the Government's main objective with respect to all claimants was to cut the rate of increase in the value of welfare payments. As intended, the result has been that the incomes of the poor have failed to rise in line with the general rise in living standards, and this policy was pursed at a time when the incomes of those in work were rising substantially. In this way the Government began its strategy of excluding a sizeable group from the substantial rise in living standards being experienced by the rest of the population. Accompanying this move has been the disenfranchisement of many from unemployment benefit, or a reduction in their entitlement to the extent already mentioned. More recently, this strategy has been given an even more sinister twist. The change in 1987 from the supplementary benefit system to income support was used to cut the money as well as the real value of state benefits. Both the reduction in the expected value of benefits, and the reduction or loss of entitlement, have undermined the effectiveness of welfare provision in ameliorating the more brutal effects of different life chances based on class. These losses of welfare entitlement have resulted in an expulsion from social citizenship as it had developed during the immediate post-war years.

Accompanying these two changes – unemployment and the linked tax and welfare strategy – has been a policy of excluding the poorest of the unskilled working class and the unemployed from acquiring a stake in the spread of private capital. The rules were carefully drafted to ensure that those on welfare were unable to buy their council houses. Similarly, those on the lowest incomes have no chance of gaining capital assets from any of the Government's privatization measures. Unemployment has also had an indirect effect on this front. Along with home ownership, the most important capital asset acquired by individuals, and sometimes more important than their home, is the right to an occupational pension. Permanent, long-term unemployment is ensuring that a large segment of the population are denied access to this form of capital.

Post-Thatcher Britain

These economic changes have been matched by equally important political developments. At the turn of the century, the terms 'working class' and 'poor' were interchangeable. Even after World War One, such interchangeability still held true for a large part of the working class. A programme aimed at ameliorating working-class conditions therefore overlapped with a programme aimed at eradicating poverty. After World War Two, particularly over the past twenty years, the more prosperous parts of the working class and those on low incomes, let alone the underclass, have increasingly held less and less in common.

The breakup of these common interests is at the centre of Labour's current political difficulties. The Labour Party was brought into existence in order to promote what were generally agreed to be the interests of the working class. What Labour now sees as being in the true interests of the working class is perceived so by less and less of what was once called the working class (for details of this whole debate, see Eric Hobsbawm, *The Forward March of Labour Halted?*, New Left Books, London, 1981). The result is that Labour's vote has, overall, continued to decline since 1951, and more markedly so in the 1983 and 1987 general elections. So, while Labour has so far found it impossible to pitch an appeal that straddles the interests it once represented, its failure to win elections has meant that it is impotent to represent the very poor as it was able to do effectively when making its traditional appeal to a more homogeneous working class. To compound its difficulties, one of Mrs Thatcher's achievements has been to turn the tradition coalition of voters' interests upside down, by making a direct appeal to the *top* 80 per cent of the electorate.

Formulating a political response requires more than designing a set of policies that will spring the underclass into freedom and back into a fraternity with other groups in British society. A political programme needs to be seen as the basis on which a political party can gain power. Discussion about a future for the underclass is therefore inextricably bound up with a discussion of post-Thatcher Britain.

If Labour and the other opposition parties are going to offer any hope for the underclass, they also need to appeal to a large number of those who feel they have profited from Thatcher's Britain. A simple appeal can be made by trying to out-bid Thatcher in terms of material success. 'But supposing unearned income, rents, etc. are pooled' observed R. H. Tawney, 'will not the world, with its present philosophy, do anything but gobble them up, and look up with an impatient grunt for more?' (*R. H. Tawney's Commonplace Book*, ed. J. M. Winter and D. M. Joslin, Cambridge, 1972, p. 61). If the appeal is only to give the snouts more to scoff up, then it is unlikely that parties of the centre and left will be more effective in their appeal than the present Conservative Party. What is also required is a programme which combines an appeal to self-interest with one of altruism. There are obvious difficulties in such an approach, but, as Jimmy Thomas once remarked to his fellow politicians: 'If you can't ride two horses at once you shouldn't be in the circus.' A riding of two horses at once requires, in part, a restatement of an ethical appeal to the electorate. It is also necessary to formulate a series of policies that have an appeal to a wider group of the electorate, but which at one and the same time play a part in a comprehensive attack on the recruiting agents and the supply routes to the underclass.

The different parts of the argument in *Losing Out* are presented in the following paper. Part I considers the pattern of class inequalities during the post-war period. Part II begins to explain, by examining the Thatcher Governments' class strategy, why class differences in Britain are now widening for the first time in post-war Britain. Part III details the six forces currently operating to fix the underclass in place. Part IV outlines a series of policies aimed at freeing the underclass by making an appeal to altruism as well as to self-interest of a wide coalition of voters.

Part I

A Cycle of Inequality

Losing Out argues that a gradual development bringing about the extension of citizenship over the past 300 years, which finally encompassed the whole population, has now been put into reverse. The status of full citizenship was not the result of a significant lessening of class differences. Rather, full citizenship was obtained despite class differences, which remained a significant feature of British life during the immediate post-war period. However, full employment and the policy of successive governments on welfare and tax did at least prevent class differences widening.

This section reviews what is known about class differences in Britain at each major point in the life cycle – in surviving birth, in benefiting from eleven years or more educational investment, in income from work, in health and in dying. The main concern will be to measure the extent to which class differences have begun to widen since 1979, in order to locate that group most vulnerable to recruitment into the ranks of the underclass. Income in Britain is related to social class. Generally speaking, the 'higher' one's social class, the greater is one's income, which itself directly affects a person's standard of living. A low income helps to explain why people in the 'lower' social classes perform less well than people from other social groups. A starting point in explaining class differences in Britain, therefore, is to examine the numbers on 'low income', to use the Government's preferred terminology, during the post-war period up to 1979. This section considers what changes have occurred since then, in order to show how the recent trends in the composition of this group have a direct bearing on the issue of the underclass.

1

The Condition of the People

Poverty Studies

The debate about who is poor in Britain has turned full circle during this century. The survey carried out by Charles Booth in London, beginning in 1887, and that of Seebohm Rowntree at the turn of the century in York, played a crucial part in establishing poverty, or, as the issue was then called, 'the condition of the people', as a political issue. Significantly, however, their findings did not support the more exaggerated claims that were circulating at the turn of the century as to the dimensions of poverty (for a fascinating discussion of this point, see Norman Dennis and A. H. Hallsey, *English Ethical Socialism*, Clarendon Press, Oxford, 1988, pp. 66–9). Many people at the time did not survive until old age, and those who did either continued working, or were taken into the workhouse. Poverty was seen largely as a 'problem' affecting those on low wages and wage earners with large families of five or more children. Writing at about the same time as the publication of these findings on the 'problem' of poverty, R. H. Tawney commented memorably: 'What thoughtful rich people call the problem of poverty, thoughtful poor people call with equal justice a problem of riches' (R. H. Tawney, Inaugural Lecture 'Poverty as an industrial problem', reproduced in *Memoranda on the Problems of Poverty*, vol. 2, William Morris Press, London, 1913).

The inter-war poverty studies changed the emphasis of concern. Most of these studies were conducted during the post-war depression and, not surprisingly, poverty was seen far less as an issue affecting large families; rather that the poor came from the ranks of the unemployed and those on low wages. However, the survey carried out just before the outbreak of World War Two, when employment was increasing rapidly, noted a change in the composition of the poor, and Rowntree's post-World War Two study reflected this emphasis (for a summary of all these surveys, see Frank Field, *Freedom and Wealth in a Socialist Future*, Constable, London, 1981, chapter 2). The effectiveness of the Coalition and Attlee Governments' welfare and full employment measures resulted in the numbers in poverty falling dramatically and the ranks of the very small minority of citizens who were poor were almost exclusively made up of pensioners. Poverty, it appeared, had been well and truly defeated by a combination of the welfare state and full employment, and consequently it had ceased to be an issue of political concern.

In the 1960s, research on the 'rediscovery' of poverty became something of a growth industry. Barbara Wootton, for example, suggested that the numbers in poverty were much larger than Rowntree had found in 1951 (see her *Social Science and Social Pathology*, Allen and Unwin, London, 1959, new edition published by Greenwood Press, London, 1978). However, it was the report *The Poor and the Poorest* published in 1965 (Bell, London) by Brian Abel-Smith and Peter Townsend that helped push poverty back onto the political agenda. While public attention was drawn to the large increase in the numbers of families who were deemed to be poor, the main group who were found to be poor in the study were the elderly. In making their calculations, the authors took the supplementary benefit rate plus 40 per cent as the dividing link between those who were and were not poor.

This is not the definition of poverty adopted here. Those living on supplementary benefit/income support are certainly on low incomes, and justice requires that their income should be higher. But it is an open question as to whether all this group can be said to be 'poor' in the sense that ordinary people would understand the term. What is crucial to this discussion is the length of time the person has been living on income support, for the longer the period, the more difficult it becomes to manage. Similarly affected are those people who are denied their full entitlement or who are paid at rates substantially below those weekly levels of most claimants.

Of course, factors other than the rates of benefits are important in determining the standard of living gained by claimants. Support from members of the extended family can play a decisive role, as does the skill at managing on slender resources. Some people have such an impressive array of these skills that they manage to remain respectable and not fall into debt. These people are to be applauded, especially as their financial acumen is probably far in advance of the rest of the population. But just as it is insulting to these people to deny the difference their skills make, it is similarly wrong to believe that most of us could match their performance if reduced to a low income.

Whatever definition is adopted, the profile of those on low incomes has changed dramatically. Overwhelmingly, those who are classified as being on low incomes today are below retirement age. Thus, the debate has turned full circle in a space of eighty years or so. Let us examine more fully the significance of this change.

Number on Low Incomes

Until they were renamed income support in April 1988, Parliament approved each year the supplementary benefit scale rates. People who are not in work, and have meagre financial resources of their own, are entitled to have their income brought up to a level prescribed by these rates. As nobody disputes that these rates give rise to only a modest standard of living, the numbers on supplementary benefit or income support can therefore be taken as a broad measurement of the numbers on low income in Britain. In the discussion that follows, all the data are based on the number of people with incomes up to the supplementary benefit level only; it does not follow the more traditional approach, and include those with incomes equal to 140 per cent of the supplementary benefit rates.

Over the entire post-war period the numbers claiming supplementary benefit have increased. From 1948 until 1979, the number of claimants on supplementary benefits (called national assistance until 1966) rose from 963,000 to 2.8 million, an increase of 1.9 million. By May 1988, the total had risen to 4.9 million. Thus, this increase of 2.1 million in nine years is greater than the increase between the establishment of the welfare state in 1948 and 1979. Even more dramatic, however, has been the increase in the numbers *dependent* upon supplementary benefit (this includes the claimant plus his or her dependents). In 1949, the total number dependent on supplementary benefit was 1.5 million, rising to 4.4 million by 1979. By May 1988, the total stood at 8.2 million. Again, the increase in the numbers of those dependent on supplementary benefit over the past nine years is far greater than the increase over the previous thirty years (note prepared by the House of Commons Library; all supplementary benefit data are from this source, unless otherwise stated).

These figures are not by themselves a full measure of those on low incomes. Large numbers of citizens appear to have incomes below the level of eligibility for supplementary benefit, but do not claim it. The size of this group can be seen from the results of the Government's special analysis of the Family Expenditure Survey (FES) data. First published in 1972, the total number living at an income below the supplementary benefit level stood at 1.8 million, falling to 1.6 million and 1.4 million respectively in the next two years. Since then, there has been a steady increase in this group up to 1983, when the total number of people living on incomes below the safety net benefit rates laid down by Parliament had reached 2.8 million. By 1985, this total had fallen back to 2.4 million. (For details of these figures, and the basis on which they were constructed, see the House of Commons Social Services Select Committee report. *Families on Low Incomes: Low Income Statistics*, House of Commons Paper 565, 1988.)

Matching the big increase in the numbers drawing supplementary benefit has been an equally important change in the *type* of person on the welfare rolls. In 1948 the overwhelming majority of claimants were pensioners. It was not until 1981 that pensioner supplementary benefit claimants were outnumbered by claimants below pensionable age, and the growth in the numbers of non-pensionable households is now so significant that, only five years later, for every pensioner claimant, there were two people below pensionable age. This change in the composition of those claiming supplementary benefit is more dramatically apparent if dependants as well as claimants are taken into account. Non-pensioners outnumbered the retired for the first time in 1976, and a decade later, for every pensioner whose living standard was determined by their supplementary pension payment, there were three below pensionable age.

The Introduction put forward the thesis that Britain's underclass is drawn from the ranks of three groups – the unemployed, single-parent families and the very old. The size of these three groups has changed over the past forty years. Unlike earlier post-war years, the vast majority of people who are now dependent on supplementary benefit are the unemployed and their families; up from 27 per cent of all claimants in 1978, to over 44 per cent in 1987 (*Hansard*, 4 July 1988, vol. 136, col. 453). Accompanying the rise in unemployment has been a large increase in the number of single-parent families. In 1970, the number of single-parent families drawing supplementary benefit stood at 191,000. This had risen to 245,000 by 1974, rising again to 300,000 by the end of the Labour Government in 1979. Over the past eight years, the numbers have doubled – up to 644,000 by May 1987 and the number of dependants stands at a little over 1 million (*Social Security Statistics*, 1987, and *DHSS Monthly Digest of Statistics*).

The decline in the proportion of pensioners drawing supplementary benefit does not mean that the number of pensioners on low incomes has fallen to an insignificant level. Rather, after a rise during the post-war period, the number of people over retirement age claiming supplementary benefit has remained almost constant over the past decade. The reason for this plateau effect is not that the number of pensioners is falling, for the reverse is in fact true, but that an increasing proportion of the growing number of pensioners now enjoy an occupational pension with which to supplement their income. Many of these same pensioners also have some savings from which they derive a small income. One concern of *Losing Out* is with the group of pensioners who have been cut off from alternative sources of income, and who are therefore totally dependent on welfare.

Another change that should be emphasized is the length of time for which people are dependent on supplementary benefit. Those pensioners who claim supplementary benefit are likely to do so until they die. It is for this reason that claimants over retirement age gained what was called the 'long-term rate', set for a married couple at 25 per cent over the ordinary rate of benefit. Under the income support scheme, pensioners gain an additional premium equal to 32 per cent of the standard benefit. We need to look at those *below* retirement age and to examine how long they remain on benefit. A further significant post-war change is the increasing number of families dependent on welfare on a long-term basis. If, for the sake of illustration, long-term dependency is measured as drawing benefit for five years, the data show more than a trebling during the six and a half years after 1979: up from 431,000 in November 1979 (the number includes dependants) to 1,345,000 by February 1986 (letter from the DHSS, 7 September 1988).

This big increase in the numbers on low income is of concern in itself, but particularly so given one of the themes developed here. Income levels are a major determinant of a person's performance throughout life – from surviving birth through and up to death – with those on low incomes at a disadvantage compared to other groups. A big increase in the numbers on low income will therefore have an afffect on the class league table, providing, of course, that the cause of the fall in income (for example, unemployment) is accurately reflected in a person's social class allocation.

Bottom 20 per cent

Why is it that the numbers on low incomes have increased, particularly in the recent past? The Government claims that the real increase in the value of supplementary benefit accounts for 40 per cent of the numbers claiming benefits since 1979. Likewise, 40 per cent of the increase in those living below the supplementary benefit level can be accounted for by the real increase in the value of supplementary benefit rates (DHSS letter to the Child Poverty Action Group, 31 December 1986). A much more significant reason has been the dramatic increase in the numbers of unemployed and, to a lesser extent, the increase in the numbers of single-parent families.

The increasing vulnerability of these two groups to low incomes can be seen from the Government's own figures on the composition of those living on incomes that bring them into the lowest quintile (the bottom 20 per cent) of the income distribution over the past fifteen years. In 1971, over half of all income-receiving units (that is, households for income support and tax purposes) in the bottom quintile were pensioners. By 1982 the proportion had fallen to around a quarter. This change is even more dramatic if people, rather than income units, are taken into account; around a fifth of the lowest quintile are now pensioners.

This change cannot be explained on the basis that the share of income going to the bottom 20 per cent has altered, for the proportion of income gained by this group has remained roughly constant. Rather, the changing composition of the lowest quintile is accounted for by the fact that, over the past thirty years, pensioners *as a group* have become significantly better off. This has occurred both in absolute terms, in that pensioners' disposable income per head has nearly tripled in real terms since 1951, and in terms relative to the rest of the population, with pensioners' disposable income per head rising from around 40 per cent of the average in 1951 to around 70 per cent today. Indeed, a considerable number of pensioners are now better off than families of working age; half of all pensioners in 1982 had incomes per head above the poorest 10 per cent in work. A quarter of them had incomes above those who were out of work (*Reform of Social Security – Background Papers*, vol. 3, Cmnd. 9519, HMSO, 1985, p. 11). However, this increase in the income of pensioners is not shared fairly. Between 1973 and 1978, old-age pensions were increased by 20 per cent in real terms, thereby benefiting all pensioners. Between 1979 and 1988, however, the national insurance pension increased by a little over 2 per cent in real terms. The continuing increase in the share of income going to pensioners has come almost exclusively from occupational pensions, from which the poorest pensioners are excluded (*Hansard*, 26 July 1988, col. 205).

Matching this increase in the absolute and relative incomes of pensioners has been a fall in the incomes of people who were previously employed. The record post-war level of unemployment 'is the single most important reason why more working-age families or income units now appear in the bottom quintile of the national income distribution than at any other time in the post-war period' (*Reform of Social Security*, p. 12). The change since 1971 has been dramatic. Unemployment accounted for a fifth of families in the lowest quintile in 1971, compared with over half of all income units in this group by 1982.

The likelihood of appearing in the bottom income range for an unemployed person is eleven times that of the equivalent individual in work; nearly twelve times greater for a married couple without children in which the husband is unemployed than for a similar couple where the husband is working; and almost eight times greater for a married couple with children in which the head is not working, than for the same family where the main breadwinner is in work.

The rise in unemployment has overshadowed the increase in the number of single-parent families that has occurred in the past fifteen years, yet the increase here has also been significant. The proportion of single-parent families in the bottom quintile has increased from 5.5 per cent in 1971 to 7.5 per cent in 1981. This change reflects the increase in the overall numbers of these families. Between 1971 and 1982 this group grew by something in excess of 50 per cent, from 607,000 to 930,000. One in 12 of families containing children were single-parent families in 1971; the proportion had changed to 1 in 8 by 1982 (*Reform of Social Security*, p. 11).

How the number of people on low income fit in with the wider picture of the total distribution of income can be seen from figure 1.1.

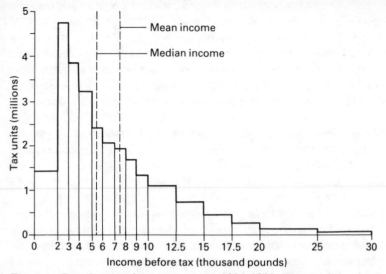

Fig. 1.1 Distribution of pre-tax incomes 1984–1985. The graph has been drawn using the following criteria: (1) the data relate to tax units (i.e. married couples and single people) in the United Kingdom; (2) 359,000 tax units with incomes over £30,000 are excluded from the graph; and (3) the area of each bar equals the number of tax units. Thus, in the lowest range, the height (1.4) times the width (2) equals the number of tax units (2.8 million).

Income on the March

Figure 1.1 gives an idea not only of the considerable number of people whose income is at the bottom end of the scale, but also of the wide variation between top and bottom. This latter point is emphasized in the verbal illustration of the pattern of income distribution, given in 1970 by the Danish economist Jan Pen. He assumed that the whole population passed before him during an hour-long procession, with the height of each person corresponding to their level of income (*Income Distribution*, Allen Lane, London, 1971). Pen's portrait of the unequal distribution of income in Britain has recently been updated by *The Economist* (26 December 1987, pp. 28–9). As the imaginary procession begins, the marchers are actually marching upside down. These are people with negative incomes, who have lost money over the previous year. Although this part of the procession takes only a few seconds, it is twice as long as it was in 1970 because there are now far more small businesses, which have a high failure rate.

Soon the first marchers appear the right way up, but they are very small – it takes about five minutes before they are even 1 foot tall. Many of these dwarf-like figures are women, working part time, although there are many more female midgets because one and a half times as many women work part time than in 1970. They are also marching with other midgets, such as single unemployed people. For nearly half of the fifth minute, we see a stream of $11\frac{3}{4}$-inch sixteen year olds, all collecting the same allowance on the Youth Training Scheme, whose 1970 equivalents in manual jobs and apprenticeships would have been about twice as tall. There are also some old faces in this part of the crowd, some of the pensioners, who in 1970 were fewer in number and pushed further back in the queue.

After twenty minutes, the marchers are still less than 3 feet tall. The few that are in full-time work are mainly women – shop assistants, cleaners and hairdressers. There are also unemployed family men and single mothers who collect benefits for themselves and their dependants.

After twenty-five minutes, most of the marchers are working, including men on full-time wages, doing farm labouring, portering and cleaning in restaurants, hospitals and offices. These low-paid workers are in the same sorts of jobs as in 1970, and their height has remained almost constant, at a little under 4 feet, although some manual workers in local authority employment have shrunk.

Half-way through the march, the marchers are still dwarves, and it is not until forty minutes have passed that people of average height (5 feet 6 inches) appear. These average marchers are people in the lower-paid professions: secretaries, postmen and so on. As the last quarter of an hour begins, we see teachers, some highly paid manual workers, bank managers, executive-grade civil servants and policemen, who have grown around 19 inches since 1970.

As the end of the march approaches, the marchers' height increases rapidly. Only one-tenth of those marching in the last ten minutes are women, and we see 10-foot journalists, 12-foot civil-service principals, some barristers and consultants 10 or 15 yards high, and merchant bankers towering hundreds of feet into the air. Still, behind these giants come some of Britain's top executives, who reach as high as the New York World Trade Centre. And in the last split seconds come those whose income is derived from inherited wealth or unearned income, such as the Duke of Westminster, whose head is invisible, 20 miles up.

The Pen description, as well as the graph, show that with so many people at the bottom of the income pile, a small change in the definition of low income or poverty will have a dramatic effect on the numbers placed in each of these categories. Mrs Thatcher, however, has done a great deal more than change the cut-off point for these definitions. She has changed the distribution itself, and for the argument in *Losing Out* it is important to note the most significant change since Pen first staged this march in 1970. There are now more 2- and 3-foot dwarves at the front of the march, but fewer of 4 and 5 feet. In contrast there are more 8- and 9-footers near the end, who passed by in the middle twenty minutes in 1970. In other words, there has been an increase in the number of those on very low incomes, but the people with whom they would historically have politically coalesced have, in increasing numbers, seen their income rise. Many of this group now see their political interest coinciding with people on even higher incomes.

Who Gains Most from Economic Growth?

Another crucial question – apart from the length of time people are trapped on low incomes, and the overall distribution of incomes – is whether those on low incomes benefit more when there is a high rate of economic growth, in terms of increases in the value of their incomes, even if this gain is 'bought' at the cost of a greater gap between them and those on average, let alone high incomes. Who gains most from a far less equal society that is growing at a record rate is a question posed by the Prime Minister as part of the defence of her economic policies.

The current rate of economic growth was discussed in the Introduction. The overall rate of growth since 1981 has been around two to three times the historic rate, and during the latter part of 1988 it was almost four times that rate. We are therefore able to test whether or not the 'trickle-down' theory works most favourably for those on low incomes during periods of rapid economic growth. Does the income of those on low income grow faster in a period of rapid economic growth even if, as a consequence, the income gap between the top and the bottom widens? That is the case advanced by the Prime Minister.

It would be extraordinary if this group notched up no gains during a period of record economic growth. The crucial question is whether they have benefited more than they did under a period of more modest improvements in living standards. The Government has recently published data showing that the relative standard of living of the poorest 10 per cent on the income scale had increased by 8.3 per cent (*Households Below Average Incomes: a Statistical Analysis*, DHSS, 1988). However, these figures should be treated with caution. First, these data are based on a very short time-span, from 1981 to 1985. Second, this improvement in living standards is from a very low base. Third, the membership of the bottom 10 per cent fluctuates significantly from year to year.

In order to obtain a more accurate picture, it is necessary to look at the 'hard-core' of those who have been dependent on minimum state benefits for long periods. The majority of the very poorest in this country are dependent upon drawing supplementary benefit/income support. At the present time, well over 8 million people are dependent on income support payments to determine their standard of living and a large proportion of this group has been dependent on benefit for a long period of time. At present over 2.5 million claimants (including pensioners) have been drawing benefit continuously for more than five years. It is on *these* people that our attention should be firmly focused.

During the period of modest economic growth, from 1970 to 1978, the value of supplementary benefit payments increased by an average of 1.1 per cent per annum in real terms. In the seven and a half years from November 1978 to April 1985, a period of much higher economic growth, the scale rate rose by only 0.7 per cent in real terms. But this average takes no account of the changes in benefit regulations, such as the 20 per cent rate contribution under the new income support system. There have also been other losses, such as regular weekly additions and the loss of single payments for most claimants. If we concern ourselves only with the rates contribution, and subtract £1.30 a week from the current rate of income support, the increase in the rate of benefit since November 1978 falls to 0.4 per cent per annum.

These figures cast considerable doubt on the view currently promoted by the Government that free-market forces not only produce a faster growth in national income, but that a richer, even if more unequal society, will better serve the interests of those on low incomes. Society is now undoubtedly better placed to do so, but this low income group has seen its living standards rise at a slower rate than when the economy was performing less effectively. This conclusion has important consequences for any discussion about ways of combating the

status of an underclass. On the record of the last decade, economic
growth by itself is insufficient. Indeed, during the period of unsur-
passed economic performance for the British economy, not only have
the living standards of those on benefit fallen further behind average
living standards, but the real increase in the value of welfare payments
is markedly less than during the period of slower economic growth.

Summary

Although the numbers on low income and the people who make up
this total are important topics in their own right, it is the most
vulnerable people within this group who are of concern in this book.
Nevertheless, all those on low incomes are more vulnerable than other
groups in the population to recruitment into the underclass, particularly as income is a major determinant of how well each of us performs
throughout life.

An overall view of the studies of the poor since the turn of the
century shows that the group in the population subjected to low
income has changed. The poverty surveys carried out by Booth and
Rowntree showed that the vast majority of people living in poverty
were on low wages, or were wage-earners with large families of five or
more children. The inter-war studies highlighted the fact that poverty
was increasingly associated with unemployment, as well as with those
on low wages. Much of the immediate post-war period was concerned
with the poverty associated with old age. More recently, however,
again due to the massive increase in unemployment, the vast majority
of those on low incomes are again below pensionable age.

During the whole of the post-war period, there was a steady increase
in the number of people whose income was so low that they were
eligible for what is now called income support. In the nine years since
1979, the number dependent on this minimum income has increased
by a greater number than the increase in the rest of the post-war
period. Amongst this record post-war total of people on low incomes,
the number of pensioners has remained almost constant. The growth
has instead been particularly significant amongst the unemployed and,
to a lesser extent, single-parent families. Moreover, as the unemployed
are excluded from work for longer and longer periods, the length of
time claimants are drawing income support has increased. It is from
the families of these two groups, the unemployed and single-parent

families, as well as those elderly pensioners on low incomes, that an underclass is emerging. As a result of its low income, the underclass fares worst with respect to the main class differences throughout life, and these are considered in the following chapters.

2

Class Differences at Birth

The chances of surviving birth provide a sensitive social indicator, and, once a baby is out of hospital, social and economic forces play an important part in determining who does and who does not reach their first birthday. Despite a fairly dramatic fall in mortality during the post-war period, significant class differences in surviving the first year of life remain. This unequal chance of surviving birth is documented in four sets of figures: the perinatal mortality rates, which cover deaths from the twenty-ninth week of pregnancy to a week after birth; the neonatal mortality rate, which covers deaths during the first four weeks of life; the post-neonatal mortality rate, which includes deaths after the first four weeks, and during the rest of the first year; and the infant mortality rate, which measures deaths in the first year of life. Each of these rates, based on internationally agreed definitions, closely reflect the health of the nation at large. The House of Commons Select Committee on Social Services remarks on the perinatal mortality rates are equally true of the other death rates listed above.

Perinatal mortality relates to a number of important social variables, such as social class and gross domestic product. . . . It has repeatedly been shown from all over the world that these rates are least where mothers are well-nourished, healthy and cognisant of the simple facts of health education. Mortality has also been shown to relate to the quality of care provided.   (First Report from the House of Commons Social Services Committee, HC 54, Session 1988–9, para. 4)

Of course, the balance of these variables changes, depending on the period under study. The physical health of the mother, which will often have been established in her early teens, is important in the period up to and immediately after the birth. Medical services are of most importance during the latter stages of the pregnancy and the period during and immediately after the birth. Once a baby has left hospital, the home environment becomes a more important factor in determining the chances of survival. Detailed information on the four different death rates of infants over the past ten years will be considered at the end of this chapter. The results of the three-part British post-war birth study are also cited, as the conclusions drawn from this survey need to be considered critically. This issue is considered in the following section, which begins by citing a survey on the trends in infant mortality during the first part of this century.

Long-term Trends

All the indices in this section make use of the classification, used by the Registrar General, of occupational groups into five main social classes. Table 2.1 sets out the different social classes, together with a separate classification for members of the armed forces. It also gives examples of the class designation for a selected group of occupations.

Table 2.1 *Social class Stratification*

Social class		Occupational examples
I	Professional	barristers, accountants, dentists, engineers, scientists, clergy, statisticians
II	Intermediate	brokers, authors, publicans, nurses, prison officers, teachers
III(N)	Skilled – non-manual	camera operators, professional sports people, draughtsmen, butchers, typists, sales representatives
III(M)	Skilled – manual	undertakers, tannery workers, weavers, bakers, printers, tailors, toolmakers
IV	Partly skilled	sewers, scaffolders, spray painters, roofers, glaziers, warehousemen
V	Unskilled	dockers, goods porters, roadmen general labourers
VI	Armed forces, inadequately described	

The first major review of all the available data that classified infant mortality along social class lines was carried out by J. N. Morris and J. A. Heady ('Mortality in relation to the father's occupation, 1911–1950', *Lancet*, 12 March 1955, pp. 554–5). They analysed the 18,000 still births and infant deaths in England and Wales between 1949 and 1950, and compared these with the data available for 1911. The authors of this report wanted to see whether class inequalities in surviving birth had narrowed during the forty-year period under study.

Their findings revealed that, although there had been a dramatic overall reduction in infant mortality, occupational and class differences remained unchanged. Of the neonatal rate for the individual occupational groups, the authors concluded that, while there had been a continuous decline in each group from 1911 to 1950, 'the fall for each occupational group is in about the same proportion'.

The authors also analysed the data according to social class. They found that: 'The rough equality of decline demonstrated for the occupational groups occurs when the occupations are grouped together into the conventional five "social classes".' And, they added: 'There has been no narrowing of the social gap in infant mortality; if anything, it may have widened slightly.'

Such findings, the authors concluded, were 'unexpected'. Why had those in social classes IV and V not improved their relative position? The most important factor, according to the researchers, was that the welfare state reforms of the 1945 Attlee Government had not been on the statute book long enough to affect basic class differences. What has been the post-war record?

Three Studies

Since the war there have been three key studies surveying children born during a specific week. The first was conducted by J. W. B. Douglas, who examined the record of all confinements in Great Britain during the first week of March 1946 (*Maternity in Great Britain*, Oxford University Press, Oxford, 1948). He made a comprehensive analysis of the life-styles and chances of this group by examining the various mortality rates of babies, according to the social class of their fathers. He noted, as had Morris and Heady, that there were considerable social class differences in death during the first week of life, and showed that approximately half the deaths were of *premature*, or low birth weight babies (that is, children who weighed 2,500 g. or less at birth).

With these findings in mind, Douglas considered which mothers were most likely to give birth to premature babies. He concluded: 'Prematurity was least common in the most prosperous groups; 4.2 per cent of all children of professional salaried workers were premature, as compared with 6.5 per cent of those black coated workers, 6.7 per cent of agricultural workers' (p. 66).

There was thus a clear correlation between social class and the death rate of infants during the first month of life. Amongst children whose fathers were classified as manual workers, the infant mortality rate was well over 50 per cent higher than for children whose fathers were professional salaried workers.

The second study was carried out on babies born in the week 3–9 March 1958 (Neville Butler and Dennis G. Bonham, *Perinatal Mortality*, E. and S. Livingstone, Edinburgh, 1965). The authors reported on the class differences of those who failed to survive birth, and they measured these differences by using what is called a mortality ratio. This is calculated as the number of actual deaths in each area or group, as a percentage of deaths that would have been expected if the local population or group being studied had experienced the sex- and age-specific mortality rates observed in the population as a whole, during the period under study.

Amongst the 17,000 children born during that particular week, it was found that: 'There is a rise from a mortality ratio of 69 in social class I to 128 in social class V. . . . [With] unmarried mothers the mortality rate for the foetus was even higher at 140 [per 1,000 births]' (p. 20).

The authors, commenting on the changes in the death rate for infants during this century, recalled the study by Morris and Heady, and remarked:

Whilst the infant mortality rate fell from 110 per 1,000 live births in 1950, the rate of each social class fell proportionately, so that relatively [*sic*] to each other, their position remained unchanged. In 1911, 1921, 1931, and 1950, the rate in social class V, unskilled workers, was roughly four times higher than in social class I, professional workers. (p. 271)

After comparing these data with the 1950 figures, the authors drew attention to the fact that:

[the] apparent widening of the gap does not merely result from changes in the extreme groups (although the relative position of class V has noticeably deteriorated) but from a general widening in disparity. Classes I and II have both improved, classes IV and V lost ground, relative to the national rate.   (p. 272)

The third study, by Roma Chamberlain and a group of colleagues, was carried out on children born during the week beginning 5 April 1970 (Roma Chamberlain et al., *British Births 1970*, Heinemann, London, 1970). The significant improvements taking place in the health of mothers and babies in the post-war period were highlighted by this study. Of the 16,749 children born during the one week covered by the study, only 421 were either stillborn or had died within one month of birth. Yet this dramatic decline in the number of infant deaths was not accompanied by a similar narrowing of class mortality differences. Once the dead infants were classified according to the occupations of their fathers, the author claimed that the reverse might be occurring: 'The most striking feature ... apart from the high perinatal mortality rate of unsupported mothers ... is the persisting steep social class gradient in mortality' (p. 17).

One explanation for this trend offered by Chamberlain was that, amongst those for whom no social classification had been made, it was possible there was a greater proportion of social class I mothers. This would account for the exceptionally low mortality rates for their babies – a perinatal mortality rate of 7.5 per cent, compared to 27.6 per cent for social class V. But even if the evidence of what happens to the babies of parents belonging to social class I is set aside, the death rate of social class II babies was: 'not much more than half that of social class V' (p. 17). More significantly, Chamberlain concluded that: 'There is nothing to contradict, and everything to support the theory that the social class differences are widening rather than diminishing' (p. 17).

A number of comments need to be made on these survey results before the conclusion on widening class differences up to the 1970s is accepted. In the first place the results in the 1946 study only give the social class background on premature births, and the number of premature babies who die. The 1958 study examined the perinatal rate – death from the twenty-eighth week of pregnancy up to the first week of life – and found a death rate amongst babies from *single mothers* (*not* social class V) of twice that for social class I babies. Because of doubts over the accurate classification of babies from social class I, the authors of the 1970 study compared the perinatal rate for social class II babies, and found that this was 'not much more than half that for social class V' babies (p. 17). The comparison of these two findings provides a somewhat shaky foundation for the study's conclusion, that there is 'everything to support the view that social class differences are widening, rather than diminishing' (p. 17).

Latest Findings

There has been no successor to these important studies. Trustees of the National Birthday Trust, who were responsible for organizing all but the first study, believed that a fourth study would not produce any significantly different findings on ways of improving medical practices from those of the previous studies, and no such study has been carried out. Since 1975, however, the Office of Population Census and Surveys (OPCS) has produced information on a consistent basis, recording all infant deaths in each year, which we do not have for the post-war period as a whole (*OPSC Mortality Statistics*, DH3 series, 1975 and subsequent years).

In order to compare the period prior to 1979 with the years following, the mortality rates for the four years from 1975 are compared with the data for the five years 1979–84. So as to counter any objections regarding the alleged smallness of social class V (see p. 35), the following analysis combines social classes IV and V, and compares the resulting rate for these two groups with that for social class I. The results are provided in table 2.2, and show a dramatic change in the post-war pattern of infant deaths. Taking infant deaths

Table 2.2 *Infant mortality rates in England and Wales, 1975–8, compared with 1979–84: Ratio Social Class IV and V to I*

	Still births (%)	Perinatal mortality (%)	Neonatal mortality (%)	Post-neonatal mortality (%)	Infant deaths (%)
1975–8	165	162	156	200	169
1979–85	174	167	161	186	169

Source House of Commons Library, Statistical Section, 4 July 1988.

as a whole, the results show a position of no improvement. However, a breakdown of the figures reveals a very different pattern: the disparities between the rates for still birth, perinatal and neonatal mortality were *greater* over the period 1979–85 than 1975–8; and the ratio for all infant deaths remained the same only because of the narrowing of the disparities in the post-neonatal mortality rates.

As was suggested above, the post-neonatal deaths are probably affected more by the quality of a child's home environment, and less by the state of medical expertise, than any of the other rates. A narrowing of class differences on this front is therefore unexpected, as the major jump in unemployment after 1979 would have led to worsening home conditions and a larger rather than a smaller disparity in survival rates. But it is crucial to remember that there is inevitably a lag before changes in the economic environment begin to affect social indicators, and this is borne out if the period since 1979 is divided into two – 1979–82 and from 1983 onwards. During the most recent period, the post-neonatal rate shows a further widening of the gap between the survival rate of babies of parents from social class I and those babies of parents from social classes IV and V (House of Commons Library, Statistical Section, 4 July 1988). This finding is very significant. The pattern to emerge under the Thatcher Governments is that, for the first time since World War Two, there is clear evidence that class differences in surviving birth are now widening.

Summary

The early part of this century was characterized by wide class differences in surviving birth. While it was expected that the social reforms of the 1945–51 Attlee Government would begin to make a major impact on relative class differences, the evidence from the three national studies indicates that this has not happened, although the conclusions about widening class differences at birth are not substantiated in the data contained in the 1958 and 1970 studies. A widening along class lines in surviving birth is, however, supported by the latest national evidence. Comparing the mortality rates of babies born over the past ten years in social classes IV and V with those born to parents in social class I, the data show a widening of the difference in surviving birth, if still births, perinatal and neonatal mortality rates are considered. It is the post-neonatal rate, which is most sensitive to changes in home conditions, where there has been a lessening of class differences in the first three years of the Thatcher Government – up to 1982. But this improvement has not been maintained. Indeed, by 1983 the effects of the major distribution favouring the richest groups, combined with the massive jump in the number of people without work, were beginning to be seen in a widening of class differences in surviving birth. The 1946 study draws attention to the additional difficulties low birth weight babies experience in surviving birth, and their greater incidence of handicap. It is significant that since 1981 both the number and proportion of low birth weight babies have increased in every year (Office of Population, Census and Survey, Monitor Series, DH3 series, 1981–2 and subsequent issues). It is from the survivors of this group of babies and particularly those born to parents in social classes IV and V that part of tomorrow's underclass will be drawn. How the disadvantage faced by this group is compounded by the educational system is considered below.

3

Educational Inequalities

Radicals and left-wingers have always attached great significance to education reform, believing that with knowledge comes power. A number of post-war studies revealed that intelligence tests, which governed entrance to grammar schools, most favoured middle-class children living in urban areas. Hence the campaign in this country to abolish the 11-plus; the belief was that this reform would lead to an equalization of outcome between children of different backgrounds. Many studies on school performance have attempted to evaluate how successful comprehensive schools have been in widening the opportunities for children from working-class backgrounds to acquire knowledge.

In this debate, all too little attention has been focused on the very poorest children, those vulnerable to recruitment into Britain's underclass. Two exceptions to this general rule are follow-up studies on the children in the 1958 National Birthday Trust study as they progressed through school. The research carried out by the National Children's Bureau (NCB) is part of the Bureau's National Child Development Study (NCDS). These studies, *Born to Fail?* and *Children in Adversity*, are of a different nature, however, to the other cited in this section. Unlike most other studies that provide a snap-shot of the performance of different children at different times, according to the social class of their parents, these two pieces of research examine in detail what happened over time to the same group of children from the most deprived homes as they progress through school.

Given the importance of the home background on a child's start in life, it is crucial to consider how quickly children have access to play and educational facilities. Are there class differences in access to pre-school education?

Unequal Before School

As with the survival chances of babies from different social classes, the evidence points to continuing class differences in attainment and the use and benefits gained from the education system. But as the NCDS observed: 'there is a sense in which the educational system itself contains a built-in bias in favour of middle-class children ... in that children from middle-class homes find in the school situation basically the same values as they experience at home.' Moreover:

By the time children start school, they have acquired an orientation to the world, embracing norms and attitudes which affect their response to school. Many working-class children will find these norms and attitudes are, in significant respects, different from those adopted by the school; they will tend to be judged by standards which are alien to their previous existence. (R. N. Davie, N. Butler and H. Goldstein, *From Birth to Seven*, Longmans, London, 1972, p. 78)

Whether or not one accepts that school values appear alien to many working-class children or, more simply, that it is because poor children generally live in the physically poorest housing and environments that makes it difficult for them to benefit fully from their schooling, pre-school activities are undoubtedly important in countering these disadvantages. However, the most disadvantaged children do not gain more favourable treatment when it comes to deciding who gets help before school life begins; in fact the reverse is the case.

The last General Household Survey to ask questions about pre-school education was carried out in 1979. The results show that the children of professional parents had the same degree of access to nursery school places as the children of semi-skilled and unskilled parents, despite the original intention that public nursery school facilities should be available for those of limited means. The children of richer parents fared even better when it came to places at a play group: 40 per cent, compared with only 24 per cent of those in the poorest homes, gained a place. Overall, 57 per cent of children under five with professional parents, in contrast to 45 per cent of children with semi-skilled and unskilled parents, had some form of day care independent of the home (*Day Care of Children Under Five*, GHS 1979, HMSO, 1981, table 6.14).

Becoming More Unequal

Pre-school education is not widely enough available to children from working-class homes to give all children an equal start at the beginning of formal education, and, perhaps not surprisingly, once children are in school, their measured ability range fluctuates according to social background. The findings of the 1946 cohort study revealed, for example, that during the primary school years the gap in attainment between children from different occupational groups begins to widen (J. W. B. Douglas, *The Home and the School*, MacGibbon and Kee, 1964, chapter 13). A similar finding is contained in the 1958 NCDS, which established a strong correlation between social class and reading and arithmetic attainment at seven years of age.

The chances of a non-skilled manual worker's child (social class V) being a poor reader are 6 times greater than those of a professional worker's child (social class I). If the criteria for poor reading are made more stringent, the disparity is much larger. Thus, the chances of a social class V child being a non-reader are 15 times greater than those of a social class I child.　(Davie et al., *From Birth to Seven*, p. 102)

Social class differences are important in understanding the recruitment to Britain's underclass. Within these trends, it is crucial to understand what happens to the poorest children. The two reports from the NCB that do just this are part of the on-going study being conducted on those children born in a single week in 1958. Researchers from the NCB interviewed the most disadvantaged children at the ages of eleven and sixteen.

While these two studies begin to lift the curtain on what life is like for the most disadvantaged of Britain's children, the timing of these interviews needs to be stressed. The researchers report on what happened to the children during a period when there was full employment, and when governments were committed to sharing the fruits of national economic growth more fairly than now. This last point cannot be too heavily emphasized, as within the existing social and economic framework it is difficult to imagine a more favourable period in economic terms for countering the disadvantages of those at the bottom of society.

While there is no general agreement about what constitutes social disadvantage, the researchers for both studies picked out three factors they believe to be of fundamental importance.

Family composition, that is five or more children in a household, or only one parent.

Low income, as defined by the supplementary benefit rates or eligibility for free school meals.

Poor housing, which was defined according to factors such as overcrowding and the lack of exclusive access to a hot water supply.

At the age of eleven 36 per cent of children were in either a single-parent family, a low-income family or were badly housed; 30 per cent of all children were from a low-income or poorly housed family; 6 per cent, or 1 in 16 of all the children, were found to be in all three of the categories singled out for this assessment of social disadvantage. Not surprisingly, these children had other handicaps as well. A significant proportion of their mothers (1 in 14) had conceived while still in their teens and many of these were heavy smokers (1 in 5). Children of young mothers, and of those who smoke, are more likely to be handicapped or to suffer poor development. This group of mothers had made less use of prenatal and antenatal care. Compared with most children, these findings reveal that the disadvantaged group, identified at the age of eleven by their social circumstances, were: 'at the time of birth, already facing substantially diminished prospects of normal development of their chances in life' (Peter Wedge and Hilary Prosser, *Born to Fail?* Arrow Books, London, 1977, p. 22).

Born to Fail?, the first report on these children, demonstrates a clear association between home circumstances and the quality of life led by many socially disadvantaged children. It requires little imagination to see how such home circumstances can severely restrict a child's chances of making the most of education.

Ninety per cent of all disadvantaged children, for example, shared a bedroom, compared with 50 per cent of 'ordinary' children. More than half of the disadvantaged children actually shared a bed, compared with only 1 in 11 of all other children. This inevitably increases the likelihood of disturbed sleep and cross-infection, which, unsurprisingly, was a great deal more common among the most disadvantaged children. Furthermore, 1 in 22 of these children both shared and wet their bed at the age of eleven. As the report dealt only with those in the sample who wet their bed, and not with any of their brothers or sisters with whom they shared, and who may also wet their beds, the figure for children sharing a wet bed must, necessarily, be significantly higher. In contrast, only 1 in about 250 of other children slept in such conditions. Put most simply, 'Even when disadvantaged children were in bed, the nature of their sleep was likely to be very different from that of ordinary children' (p. 26).

These disturbed nights, and the other aspects of life in a disadvantaged home, were generally reflected in the health of such children, and in their performance at school. These disadvantaged children visited welfare clinics less often and were less likely than their peers to be immunized against severe illness. According to their mothers, the disadvantaged children were more likely than normal children to be absent from school due to illness. One in 11 were absent for between one and three months, and 1 in 50 for more than three months during the year prior to their eleventh birthday. These figures compared with 1 in 25, and 1 in 250 respectively amongst other children (p. 40).

The difficult home backgrounds and the poor health records of these children were reflected in their school results. Not only did fewer disadvantaged children have any pre-school education, but, once at school, performance differences, rather than diminishing, became more marked. By the age of eleven, the disadvantaged children were some three and a half years behind ordinary children in their reading scores.

This average does, however, disguise the success of some children from disadvantaged backgrounds. One in 7 gained higher reading scores than half of the non-disadvantaged group. Similar results were registered in mathematics (p. 53). How did these gifted and not so gifted children from disadvantaged backgrounds fare in secondary schools?

The researchers returned to interview the children when they reached the age of sixteen by which time some of those classed at age eleven as disadvantaged according to the three criteria above were no longer so. Their places had, however, been taken by other children. *Children in Adversity*, the follow-up study, details the many difficulties that socially disadvantaged children encounter that are alien to the experience of ordinary, let alone privileged children (Peter Wedge and Juliet Essen, *Children in Adversity*, Pan Books, London, 1982). These acutely disadvantaged children came from homes run by a parent or parents on welfare, who were more likely to be disabled, sick, unemployed or all three. When their fathers, and sometimes their mothers, were in work, they were more likely to be in the lowest paid jobs. For part of their lives, some of the children had been taken away from their parents.

What then of the attainment of such children at school? Teachers were asked if their pupils could undertake those calculations required for everyday shopping, and read well enough to cope with the ordinary needs of everyday life: 'Easily the largest proportion of those who were said to be unable to do each of these [tasks] was among the long-term disadvantaged' (p. 66). Seven times as many disadvantaged as ordinary children could not meet the basic requirements on calculations, and ten times as many had reading abilities that failed to meet the modest target requirement.

All of the children were tested in maths, reading and comprehension. The results showed that the long-term disadvantaged had slightly lower average scores than those children who were found only to be disadvantaged at age eleven. The scores of this latter group were, however, closer to the long-term disadvantaged than to ordinary children. 'This confirms . . . that children who have been in adverse circumstances, such as poor housing or one-parent families, tend to have relatively poor attainments at 16, even if their conditions have improved by then' (p. 68).

This finding needs to be stressed, for it appears that a child's performance is affected by a disadvantaged background, and this affects performance, even when the source of disadvantage is removed. As the researchers remarked: 'This is . . . of considerable importance, given that only a small proportion of children is disadvantaged at any particular age, compared with those disadvantaged at some stage of childhood' (p. 73).

Despite the belief of some people to the contrary, it is crucial to stress the finding that these results do not suggest that a child's relatively poor school record is an indication of a low level of ability rather than his or her social circumstances. The comparison of the progress of children with different ability levels: 'revealed no evidence that disadvantaged children who started secondary school with good test results were disproportionately likely to make poor or not poor progress relative to ordinary children; their progress appeared to be hindered to the same extent as disadvantaged children with poor initial ability' (p. 73).

As the abilities of the children had been tested at eleven, it was possible to compare the results of *Born to Fail?* and *Children in Adversity*. It is clear from these results that the present educational system alone does not lessen inequalities in life chances, or prevent the further growth of Britain's underclass – rather the reverse is true. Put simply, disadvantage accumulates during adolescence, and the 'differences that exist when they were 11 increase during the secondary school period' (pp. 71, 73).

Almost the only encouraging finding in the whole report was that some of the disadvantaged children, against all odds, were found to be high attainers. Of these, a third were disadvantaged at the age of eleven only, compared with 21 per cent of those disadvantaged at both the age of eleven and sixteen. No significant difference emerged either when an examination was made of the likelihood of this group belonging to a single-parent family. What was found, however, was that those schools attended by disadvantaged high attainers tended to include a higher proportion of middle-class children, compared with the schools of other disadvantaged children (p. 79).

It is not clear from these results whether these schools, on the whole, were better run and motivated, or whether the crucial factor was the nature of the parental choice of school in the first place. Did these parents fight harder to get their children into better schools in the neighbourhood, thereby denoting their particular and possibly continuing interest in their child's education?

While *Children in Adversity* does not address itself specifically to this question, it seems to confirm that at least one of the crucial explanations for a disadvantaged child's attainment, like that for all high attainers, is parental interest and encouragement. For most disadvantaged children: 'neither their own nor their parents' aspirations for the future were as high as the rest of their peers' (p. 81).

The role of parents in the success of their children's schooling is clearly crucial. The focus of analysis needed to understand significant variations in educational attainment between social classes therefore ultimately needs to extend beyond the classroom.

Summary

The two NCB studies on the performance of the very poorest children were carried out during the exceptional decades of this century – the period of full employment when, as will be seen in the following discussion, income was distributed more equally than at any other time. The NCB's longitudinal study showed that the group of children suffering the most disadvantage in home life did less well at school; the performance differences between the poorest children and other children, continued to widen by the time the children were eleven, and at the age of sixteen the disadvantages faced by these children had had a cumulative impact. These studies also reveal that the performance of those children who were amongst the most disadvantaged for only part of their lives was none the less affected in the long term by their temporary experience of disadvantage. Moreover, the differences in educational attainment between the most and least privileged children cannot be adequately explained by differences in ability levels. The reader is left to surmise what the performance of the least privileged children is today, when income and class differences are at a record post-war high. We now turn to examine how these inequalities at birth and in school are reinforced in the labour market.

4

Income Inequalities

The most disadvantaged children in the 1958 National Child Development Study left school in 1964, a decade or more before the
significant increase in the numbers of unemployed. These entrants to
the job market would have gained low-paid, dead-end jobs. The
majority of the most disadvantaged children and young people leaving
school today will not find a job. They either become unemployed or
gain a place on a Youth Training Scheme (YTS), although a sizeable
number will then gain work, but on low pay. This chapter considers
what has happened to the earnings of the poor in work, which is
usually measured by the pay going to the lowest decile – that is, the
poorest 10 per cent. The analysis is taken from the New Earnings
Survey (NES), which is an annual report on the earnings of different
groups in the population. Earnings also make up a significant part of a
person's total income, and this chapter also considers what has
happened to the distribution of income during the post-war period.

The Earnings Record

Figures on the dispersion of weekly earnings of male manual workers
were first collected in 1886. In that year, the wages paid to the lowest
decile stood at 68 per cent of median earnings. Data were again
collected in 1906, when the value of the lowest decile's wages, as
compared to the median, fell to 66.5 per cent. It is only since 1963 that
earnings surveys have been conducted annually, although in 1982 a
small change was introduced into the computation of the data.

The results of these surveys show that, until recently, the value of
the pay of the lowest decile had not fallen below 67.3 per cent of

median earnings, and had not risen above 71.6 per cent: a dispersion of 4 percentage points. The size of the dispersion needs to be kept in mind when reviewing recent change. Indeed, as though to emphasize the point, the *Department of Employment Gazette* commented that the dispersion of manual men's earnings: 'has changed little, particularly at the lower end, over the period from 1886 to the present day' (October 1981, p. 446).

So, once again, until recently, the position on earnings has been not dissimilar to other measurements of British society, with marked differences – often reflecting those of social class – but of no deterioration in the relative position of those at the bottom of the hierarchy. However, the most recent NES results show a marked change. The pay of the lowest decile of male manual workers in 1979 stood at 68.3 per cent of median earnings. By 1987, this had fallen to 61.9 per cent – the lowest recorded value at any point since the NES began collecting data in 1963, and, in a wider historical perspective, since records were first collected in 1886. An even more significant decline is apparent if the poorest non-manual male workers are considered separately. In 1979, their pay stood at 63.4 per cent but had fallen to 55.9 per cent by 1987.

Despite the fact that women workers have had the protection of the Equal Pay Act, designed to increase their pay as a proportion of men's earnings, many low-paid women have also seen a decline in their relative earnings. The pay of the poorest 10 per cent of manual women workers stood at 75.5 per cent of the median in 1979, and was down to 72.3 per cent in 1987. The lowest decile of non-manual women workers' pay records a similar decline to that of their male colleagues, down from 69.2 per cent of median earnings to 64.6 per cent since Mrs Thatcher took office in 1979. Overall, combining the pay of manual and non-manual workers, the value of the poorest 10 per cent's pay against median earnings records a 7.4 percentage points decline over the past seven years for male workers, and a 6 percentage points decline for women workers.

A contrary trend is discernible for the pay received by the highest paid workers. The pay of the top 10 per cent, manual and non-manual men alike, shows a steady drawing away from those on average, let alone low pay. Combining the pay for both sets of male workers, we see that, in the eight years since 1979, the highest decile of gross earnings as a proportion of median earnings has risen by a staggering 22.2 percentage points (all data from *New Earnings Survey*, 1987, table 31).

It is important to note that these are gross earnings. Later we shall look at the tax changes since 1979, and at how these have overwhelmingly benefited those who are already on high pay, thereby reinforcing the changes brought about by the market and affecting the pay of those at the top and the bottom of the earnings league.

Here it is important to note the significance of the changes that have occurred since 1979. The previous pattern of income distribution, where differences were marked, but were kept within set bounds, has been shattered. Since the end of the 1970s, the earnings of those at both ends of the earnings scale have moved sharply away from the average. This is obviously a boon to those already on high earnings. For those at the bottom of the scale, this tendency represents a bad situation that is becoming steadily worse. Earnings are, however, only one part, albeit an important one, in determining a person's income. We now turn to consider some of these wider issues.

Widening Income Gap

Unlike the new NES data, the official data on the distribution of income cover, for example, not only wages and salaries, but income from interest, rents, dividends and professional fees, and all social security benefits liable to tax. As these data are gathered from tax returns, they are presented on the basis of tax units, which often cover more than one person – most husbands and wives are taxed as a single unit. The number of tax units, for example, is 29 million, while at the same time there are some 40 million adults, living in around 20 million households. How has the pattern of income distribution changed during the post-war period, and has there been a marked change since 1979?

In 1949, the top 1 per cent of income earners cornered 11.2 per cent of pre-taxed income. By 1978–9, this had been halved to 5.3 per cent. The fall in the share going to the top 2–5 per cent was far less marked: it fell from 12.6 to 10 per cent over the same period. A similar picture merges for the richest 10 per cent. Their income share before tax moved from 33.2 per cent in 1949, to 26.1 per cent in 1978–9, the year before Mrs Thatcher came to power.

It was this move towards a greater income equality that gave Mrs Thatcher her greatest concern, for she believed it stifled enterprise, which is the driving force behind the free market system. Much government effort was therefore put into reversing this post-war trend. Moreover, while governments can have a direct effect on the distribution of post-tax income, in ways that are spelt out in Part II, their influence on its pre-tax distribution is much more indirect and subtle. This indirect effect has, however, been brought fully into play, resulting in the reversal of the long-term trend towards greater equality of pre-taxed income. The richest 1 per cent's share rose from 5.3 per cent in 1978–9, to 6 per cent in 1981–2, and to 6.4 per cent in 1984–5, the latest data available. Similar gains are notched up for the top 6–10 per cent. The richest 10 per cent's share of pre-taxed income has risen from 26.1 per cent during the last year of the Labour Government, to 29.5 per cent in 1984–5.

The poorest 10 per cent's share of pre-tax income stood at 2.2 per cent in 1966, the first year in which separate data for the lowest decile were published. This rose to 2.5 per cent in 1970–1, and 2.7 per cent in 1973–4. It then declined, falling to 2.5 per cent in 1975–6, 2.4 per cent in 1978–9, and 2.0 per cent in 1981–2, but rising to 2.3 per cent in 1984–5. The share of the next decile, the 81–90 quintile, reveals a constant position of 3.5 per cent from 1978–9 onwards (Blue Book Statistics and the New Income Series in *Economic Trends*, November 1987, table A, p. 94).

The view that the British tax system acted as an equalizing force on income distribution in the earlier post-war period is confirmed by the official data. The share of the top 10 per cent of income groups fell, after tax, from 27.1 per cent in 1949, to 23.1 per cent in 1975–6. This rose very slightly to 23.4 per cent in 1978–9. The big change in the distribution of income is recorded after 1979, with the share of the top 10 per cent rising to 25.6 per cent in 1981–2. No such improvement is recorded for the poorest 10 per cent's income share, which dropped from 3.2 per cent in 1973–4 (the first year in which separate data were published) to 3.0 per cent in 1975–6, 2.9 per cent in 1978–9, and 2.4 per cent in 1981–2.

Latest Trends

A serious objection to using the official data to measure changes in income shares over time is that they take no account of the changing size of households. Michael O'Higgins, in an important article, reworks the official data on the basis of what is called net equivalent income, whereby net income is recalculated to assume the equal size of the household ('The distribution and redistribution of income in the UK, 1971–84', in *New Priorities in Public Spending,* ed. M. S. Levitt, Gower, London, 1987). His analysis can be used to consider, first, the distribution of market income, which is composed of earned income, together with investment income, occupational income and the like; and, second, the distribution of net income, which is made up of market income plus cash transfers, but less tax and National Insurance contributions.

The data show the profound extent to which unfettered market forces have generated increasingly large inequalities of income. Starting from a 1971 base, the distribution of market income shows: 'a pattern of increasing inequality throughout the period, with increases in the share of the top quintile [20 per cent] especially rapid after 1979' (p. 55).

The bottom 20 per cent of the income pile had almost no income from work, even by 1979. Even so, the significance of recent gains for top income earners is shown by the fact that while in 1971 the market share of the top 20 per cent was less than 3.5 times that of the bottom 40 per cent cent, 'in 1984 it was more than 7.5 times greater' (p. 55). Most of this change was brought about by earnings rather than changes in unearned income or occupational pensions.

For reasons outlined above, the relative fall of those at the bottom of the distribution cannot be explained by an increasing proportion of pensioners on low income making up this section of the earnings distribution. The proportion of adults in the bottom quintile who were retired fell from more than three-quarters in 1976 and 1979, to just over half in 1984. The places of these pensioners who, thanks to occupational pensions, found themselves placed in a higher income group, were taken by the long-term unemployed.

This picture changes once the effect of taxes and benefits is taken into account. The distribution of net income, over the period 1971–84, indicates a consistent improvement in the position of the top quintile (see table 4.1 on p. 53 of *New Priorities in Public Spending*). It is important to remember that this change in the distribution may be accounted for by changes in the size of the households being studied. In order to take into account the different needs and earning abilities of households of different compositions, O'Higgins also reworked the net income data, so as to present them in the form of equivalent income shares (that is, the relative living standards of each 20 per cent

of the population). These data help identify the periods when changes
were due to alterations in the compositions of households, rather than
to other factors.

Between 1971 and 1976, the income share of the top 20 per cent
fell, while that of the bottom 20 per cent increased. From 1976 to
1979, the direction of these changes was reversed, although on a scale
only half that of the preceding period. From 1979, the top and bottom
20 per cent gained 'though the gain is almost 3 times greater at the top'
(p. 53). There is little further change during the period 1982–4, and
O'Higgins concludes that 1979 was the turning point in recent years
for this change in the distribution of income (p. 53).

The top 5 per cent are singled out for special consideration, as this
'allows one to distinguish what is happening to the "genuinely
affluent"' (p. 51). Between 1971 and 1979, the share in net income for
the top 5 per cent records a fall (down from 13.8 per cent in 1971, to
13.2 per cent in 1979) followed by a sharp rise from 1979 to 1982
(p. 61). Indeed, after 1979, it is the gain of the top 5 per cent that
accounts for the changed circumstances of the whole of the top 20 per
cent (the next 15 per cent lost ground during this period).

Reviewing the whole period, O'Higgins concludes that the net
income data point to:

a widening in measured inequality from 1971 to 1976 which was due to
changes in household composition and in fact concealed a decrease in the
inequality of the distribution of living standards. From 1976 to 1979,
inequality increased somewhat, but the gainers in the top two quintile groups
did not include the top 5 per cent of households. Between 1979 and 1982, the
bottom quintile and the top decile, in particular the top 5 per cent,
gained.   (p. 55)

O'Higgins is clear on the reasons for this change. We have seen how
important market income is in determining the final outcome of
income shares. It is the *'reduced access to market income* which explains
recent increases in inequality' (p. 63, emphasis added).

O'Higgins also found that, of the years falling within the scope of his
study, the net distribution of income was most *equal* in 1976, and it was
at this point that the ratio of market income to net income was at its
highest. 'The inequalities generated by a market which provides
employment to all who seek it are smaller than those which arise when
part of the population is forced to rely on social transfers' (p. 63).

Put simply, these two conclusions mean that the most effective policy for countering inequality of income is to increase people's access to market income, or, in everyday terms, to increase radically the numbers in work. It was at the high point of the post-war period of full employment that market and net incomes were most equal. In other words, no tax regime has been as effective in bringing about greater equality of income as a policy of guaranteeing full employment – or, at least, no tax regime that has been used with the determination demonstrated by Mrs Thatcher in her use of the full range of fiscal measures at her disposal.

Summary

Earnings and incomes provide a further link in the pattern of growing class division in Britain. The picture on both counts is similar, with the slow post-war move towards greater equality of reward being firmly reversed in recent years, particularly since the election of the first Thatcher Government in 1979. Two trends are evident with respect to earnings. The gap between the poorest worker's wages and those on average wages has widened to an all-time record. Another record gap has opened between the earnings of those on top pay and the average. With respect to income, in 1971, the richest 20 per cent had an income of less than three and a half times that of the poorest 40 per cent of the population. By 1985, the difference had increased to seven and a half times. The income and earnings data also underline how important the level of employment is for influencing the degree of economic inequality in society, a matter that is discussed further in Part IV. The figures for 1976 – that is, before the spiralling unemployment of the Thatcher years – record the smallest difference between the distribution of market income and the final income that people are left with in their pockets and purses. This information on income is central to the argument of *Losing Out*. While differences in income represent a major inequality in their own right, they also affect life chances in a fundamental way. Income differences underlie the varying chances of surviving birth discussed in chapter 2. Marked income differences also help to explain why some people die so much earlier than others. This is the issue to which we now turn.

5

Health Inequalities

In surviving birth, in education and with regard to income, the post-war pattern is the same: no closing of class differences, and, generally speaking, from 1979 onwards, a widening of the class divide. The prevailing view is that the pattern is different with respect to health, in that it is claimed that class differences have widened throughout the post-war period, rather than just since 1979. The evidence supporting this view is critically reviewed in this section, which begins by drawing on the Registrar General's decennial reports, and the conclusions that have been drawn from them by the Black Report (*Report of the Working Group on Inequalities in Health*, DHSS, 1980). This is now a highly charged political debate, and it is on this note that this chapter begins.

Long-term Differences

Little specific information on ill health is collected in this country, and, in the absence of such data, ill health is measured in terms of morbidity (death rates). Particularly important for this study are the main differences in the death rate for each of the main social groups, and, in particular, the degree to which the class rates vary from what is called the *standard mortality ratio*. This is calculated by examining the extent to which death rates for certain conditions for people from different social classes compare with the national average for those conditions.

The extent to which the standard mortality ratio varies according to different social classes is an issue that has drawn comment in official publications, and has also been highlighted by senior politicians. In 1977, for example, the then Secretary of State for Social Services expressed his concern about the crude differences in mortality rates between different classes, observing:

to take the extreme example, in 1971, the death rate for adult men in social class 5 (i.e. unskilled workers) was nearly twice that of adult men in social class I (professional workers), even when account has been taken of the different age structures of the two classes. When you look at the death rates of public diseases, the gap is even wider. For example, for tuberculosis, the death rate in social class 5 is 10 times higher than that for social class I; for bronchitis, it is 5 times as high, and for lung cancer, 3 times as high.   (speech by David Ennals, 27 March 1977)

Following this speech, the Social Services Secretary requested that his chief scientist appoint a working group to assemble the available information about differences in health status amongst different social classes. This report, known as the Black Report after its chairman, Sir Douglas Black, was ready for publication in 1980, but it was at this point that the Government moved to hush up the working party's findings. Indeed, the newly elected Conservative Government was so unhappy with the report's findings that it refused to have the report printed. Instead, it made 260 typescripts available on the August Bank Holiday Monday of that year. As the Government evidently intended the debate to end on that bank holiday, a comment in the preface to the report by the then Secretary of State for Social Services, Patrick Jenkin, is very striking. Jenkin wrote of the: 'disappointment to many that over long periods since the inception of the NHS, there is generally little sign of health inequalities in Britain actually diminishing and, in some cases, they may be increasing' (Foreword to *Report of the Working Group on Inequalities in Health*).

The conclusions of the Registrar General's regular reports on morbidity, the Black Report into class differences in mortality and more recently published evidence all bear grim witness to the pervasive nature of disadvantage.

A Black Picture

Every decade the Registrar General produces the definitive study on death rates in this country. Particularly important is his analysis of the variations in the death rate along class lines. Once again, we make use of the most common classification, which divides the population into five main social groups, with a sub-division of social class III, and a separate classification for all those in the armed forces.

At regular intervals, changes are made in the allocation of occupational groups to the different social classes. While these changes may affect only a minority of occupations, changing class allocation of different occupations makes the use of morbidity data a hazardous exercise, especially when the data stretch over long periods. Indeed, the Registrar General remarked in his 1961 report that it was 'impossible to disentangle real differential changes in mortality in this context, from apparent differences due to changes in classification' (*Decennial Supplement for 1961*, HMSO, 1971, p. 22). The changes in classification that took place in 1960 led to approximately 26 per cent of occupations being allocated to a different social class than the one to which they were assigned in the 1950 classification.

The Registrar General did not, however, rule out all time-sequenced comparisons – he published two such examples. The first showed that, by taking select professional groups, such as doctors, teachers and lawyers, 'not all of the improvement in social classes I and II is due to differences in classification' (*Decennial Supplement for 1961*, pp. 22, 27). Second, he recorded that the most disturbing feature of the 1961 results, when compared with earlier analyses, was the apparent deterioration in social class V. Even when the rates are adjusted to the 1950 classification, it is clear that class V men fared worse than average (p. 29).

In his following report, covering occupational mortality during the period 1970–2, the Registrar General concluded that, overall, there was little change in the relative mortality advantage that members of social classes I and II continued to enjoy relative to other classes. Reviewing the whole post-war period, however, the Black Report came to a rather different conclusion.

First, the report suggested that there was a greater inequality of mortality between occupational classes I and V, both in 1970–2 and 1959–63, than in 1949–53 (*Report of the Working Group on Inequalities in Health*, p. 71). Second, between 1959–63 and 1970–2, the mortality rates of different age groups over thirty-five in occupational class III and classes IV and V combined 'either deteriorated, or showed little improvement: and, relative to the mortality rates of occupational classes I and II, they worsened' (p. 71). Third, excluding those in social class I, who account for less than 1 per cent of married women, 'the data ... show the same "spread" of mortality for married and single women as for men. For both married and single women in class V, mortality increased relative to women generally during the 1960s' (p. 71).

These conclusions of the Black Report – showing widening class differences in mortality for the whole of the post-war period – have come in for some stringent criticism, particularly from Julian Le Grand and Raymond Illsley (see 'The measurement of inequality in health', a paper given to the Annual Meeting of the British Association of Science, September 1986). After looking at the kind of data presented in the Black Report, which made comparisons over the past four decades, and, as has been seen, asserted a widening of class differences, Le Grand and Illsley remark that 'it is the *interpretation* of these facts, and not the facts themselves, that is disputed' (p. 3, emphasis added). In interpreting the data, the authors maintain that there are three main issues that must be considered.

The first is how the interpretation of these statistics relates to the measurement of social class.

The need exists for a measure which summarises the individual's experience of poverty, wealth and standards of living. Over long periods, this is not available, and, as a proxy indicator, individuals are allocated to their occupational category, and that category is then grouped with others to form a 'class'. Not only is this group measure a very indirect indication of the individual's experience, but also it is not self-evident that, in comparing class I in 1921 with class I in 1981, and in comparing each with its class V counterpart, that we are comparing like with like. The measuring rod may change, and our results may reflect that change rather than any change in group health.　(pp. 3–4)

The critics have a fair point here. The authors also maintained that there is a further problem, centring on the meaning and measurement of inequality

If equality is measured on the basis of differences between social groups (or socio-economic classes), is greater equality achieved if the size of the affluent (healthy) groups increase as a proportion of the population, and the poor (unhealthy) decline? Or does inequality persist unchanged if the death rates of the extreme classes remain in the same relationship, even though the lowest class may have decreased to a small minority, whilst the highest class has multiplied?　(p. 4)

A further difficulty, according to Le Grand and Illsley, derives from the mechanics by which inter-class mobility takes place. They maintain that, broadly speaking:

those who rise from lower classes do so because their environment or upbringing is favourable: this is reflected in their social, physical and intellectual growth and development. Their departure from the lower classes is accompanied by a downward movement from those in the upper classes whose micro-environment has been less favourable. There thus occurs a constant inter-class exchange, which serves to reinforce the characteristics of both classes. The net result, in terms of outcome, depends upon the amount and direction of movement, and the severity of selection. Providing selectivity remains the same, higher social mobility is thus likely to produce greater class inequality. Since the factors which encourage upward social mobility are also favourable to health (and vice versa) the continuous stream of inter-class movement reinforces class differences and the class gap in health. (pp. 6–7)

In making these points, Le Grand and Illsley are particularly concerned to challenge the view that the National Health Service can be judged to have 'failed' because the figures suggest no lessening of social class differences in health and mortality. Their argument, in essence, is that, as the groups that are allocated to each social class change over time, no sound conclusions can be drawn from class morbidity and mortality rates, and hence that the arguments about the effectiveness of the NHS may be groundless. This was politically a perceptive line of thought. The evidence in the Black Report could have been used in the current debate about the future of the NHS. The apparent failure of the service to reduce class differences in mortality could have become a powerful argument for recasting the health service.

Yet, paradoxically, the more persuasive Le Grand and Illsey are in the case they marshall against the interpretation of the data in the Black Report, the more inevitable is the emergence of an underclass. Indeed, the authors' own argument on social mobility, which is more than faintly reminiscent of social Darwinism, would suggest that the emergence of such an underclass is inevitable. The puzzle, from their angle, can only be that it has taken so long for such a phenomenon to become discernible.

Missing Information

There we leave this particular argument, with Le Grand and Illsey so far getting the better of it. What is crucial to *Losing Out* are the recent trends in class differences in morbidity. While accepting the main thrust of Le Grand and Illsley's argument regarding the dangers of making sweeping comparisons on social class differences in mortality over long periods of time, the debate here is much more narrowly time-scoped. Making a more limited analysis is something the Registrar General has done himself, although significantly not in the latest report (*Occupational Mortality: The Registrar General's Decennial Supplement for Great Britain, 1979–80, 1982–3*, HMSO, 1986). This report is, however, important for the support its data give to the assertion made in *Losing Out* that class differences have begun to widen since 1979. The report does not, of course, only examine changes since Mrs Thatcher's first election win. It *does* report on mortality differences during 1980–2, and this allows some class comparisons to be made with the 1970–2 report. However, as the *British Medical Journal* noted: 'something strange has happened – reference to the social class differences in mortality have almost slipped out' ('Lies, damned lies and suppressed statistics', *BMJ*, 9 August 1986, pp. 349–50). The *BMJ* went on to consider why this should be the case. 'Could it be because someone in the Government or in the Registrar General's Office is anxious to play down the widening gap in mortality between rich and poor?' (p. 349).

In the Introduction, reference was made to the extent to which the 1970–2 Registrar General's report included a sixty or so page consideration of social class differences in mortality. In contrast, the 1980–2 report had only five pages concerned with an analysis of death according to social class. The *BMJ* editorial claims:

the commentary gives only passing reference to the [social class] figures and then principally to emphasise their weakness. The report claims that the figures for social class V are unreliable, and that we should look elsewhere for a more authoritative account of recent differences in mortality among social classes. This statement is surprising enough, but even more striking is the absence of any detailed analysis of what has gone wrong, and how to overcome the problem.   (p. 349)

As the *BMJ* editorial observes, the 'serious reservation' that the Registrar General has in comparing these latest results with those of earlier censuses suggests that such differences in comparison have been met before, and more importantly, overcome. As has been seen, efforts were made in previous reports to devise bridging mechanisms, so that comparisons could be made over time. This led the *BMJ* to remark that the latest decennial supplement 'could and should have been used to answer the question "have any inequalities in health widened?"' (p. 350).

In an attempt to overcome any distortion created by the changes made to the social class V classification, the *BMJ* suggested a way whereby 'a simple and valid comparison' with earlier data could have been made. Table 5.1, which reproduces the *BMJ* table, shows that the differences between social classes I and V have in fact widened, if the first five years of Mrs Thatcher's administration are compared with the class morbidity results recorded in 1970–2. 'The mortality rate of men higher up the social scale has improved, and that of those lower down the scale has deteriorated' (p. 350).

Table 5.1 *Comparison between standard mortality ratios in 1970–1972 and 1979–1983*

Social class	Standard mortality ratios, 1970–2			Standard mortality ratios, 1979–83		
I	77 ⎫ 80			66 ⎫ 74		
II	81 ⎭	⎫ 86		76 ⎭	⎫ 80	
III(N)	99	⎬		94	⎬	
III(M)	106	⎭		106	⎭	
IV	114 ⎫ 121	112		116 ⎫ 129	116	
V	137 ⎭			165 ⎭		

Source *British Medical Journal*, **293**, 9 August 1986.

Much of the 'missing' class-based information was carried in an issue of the *Lancet* the same week that the Registrar General's report was published (M. G. Marmot and M. E. Dowan, 'Mortality decline and widening social inequalities', *Lancet*, 2 August 1986). As one of the authors of this article worked in the Registrar General's office, it is possible to speculate about the internal argument that must have taken place when the bulk of the section on class difference in mortality was jettisoned from the officially published data. The *Lancet* article carried a report of an examination of death from all causes, and noted the incidence of lung cancer, coronary heart disease and cerebro-vascular disease, or strokes.

The figures for the first four years of the Thatcher Government (1979–83) were compared with the Registrar General's published data for 1970–2. Mortality from all causes during the 1979–83 period fell relative to this earlier period in non-manual and manual groups for both men and women. This fall, however, has not been evenly spread among social classes. In fact: 'the social gradient has widened: mortality has declined more rapidly among non-manual than among manual groups' (p. 275).

The data were also analysed according to specific causes of death. Mortality rates from cerebro-vascular disease and lung cancer 'show a similar picture' to the overall trend. Deaths from lung cancer in women, and coronary heart disease in men and women have fallen in non-manual groups: 'but in those classified as manual [occupations], mortality has risen over the decade' (p. 275).

An analysis according to age shows 'non-manual workers to be favoured more at younger than at older ages' (that is, class differences were becoming more marked over time), and for each cause group (for example, lung cancer) and each age group, 'their relative advantage has increased over time'. The mortality rate for heart disease was also considered on a geographical basis, and this showed a decline in mortality in non-manual groups in every part of the country, although such a decline was marginal in Scotland. In contrast, the standard mortality ratios for manual workers 'have stayed roughly constant in every region but Wales', were there was a significant fall. The researchers concluded: 'regional differences in mortality have changed little over the decade' (p. 275).

The authors considered a number of reasons why their findings might be unreliable. Whether, for example, the dramatic results might be explained by changes in disease classification, or social class composition, or by environmental or lifestyle factors affecting classes to varying degrees. They concluded, however, that changes in social class or occupational classification were an inadequate explanation for: the steeper decline in all-cause mortality for those belonging to non-manual groups; the widening class differences in death associated with specific causes; the worst relative position of those in manual groups; or the deteriorating relative position of those in social classes IV and V. On the contrary: 'the reverse is more usual, and this bias would be likely to reduce social class differences' (p. 275).

The authors suggest that unemployment may be the causal factor in the worsening position of those at the bottom of the social hierarchy. 'It is possible that worsening unemployment, selectively affecting manual occupations, causes a true rise in the mortality of manual occupations, relative to non-manual occupations' (p. 275).

On income differentials between manual and non-manual groups, which have already been reviewed (see chapter 4), and which have widened since 1979, the authors commented: 'To the extent that income *per se* accounts for part of the inverse association between social class and mortality, a widening gap in income between classes might play some part in the widening gap in mortality rates' (p. 276).

Summary

There is intense dispute amongst academics over the interpretation that should be given to the morbidity statistics over the last seven decades. This argument is less important in respect to the more recent period, which shows a widening of class differences in morbidity if data from the first four years of Mrs Thatcher's Government are compared with the Registrar General's report for the period 1970–2. The underlying cause of this change is the rise in unemployment, which was more gradual during the mid-1970s, and very rapid from 1979 to 1982, and the simultaneous increase in income differences, again gradual in the 1970s, and more significant after 1979.

Conclusion

A widely shared assumption in this country has been that, from World War Two up until 1979, Britain had become a more equal society in terms of income, as well as more generally in terms of life chances. The evidence that has been presented in Part I puts a serious question mark against the accuracy of this interpretation of social trends. It is true that, initially, the evidence on income and wealth supports the view of a growing equality in the distribution of rewards – although space has not allowed any criticism of the accuracy of the official figures. But on all other fronts, an uneasy class truce was maintained by the promotion of full employment and bipartisan social and economic policies. This consensus has been rudely broken, in particular by Mrs Thatcher's drive to make the distribution of income and wealth ever more unequal. The extent and consequences of the changes brought about by the Prime Minister's approach should not be underestimated. The evidence reviewed in this section illustrates how the crucial determinant of class differences – changes in income levels – has already led to a widening of the dispersion of life chances; on surviving birth, on earnings and income, on health and morbidity.

It was argued in the Introduction that class differences were compatible with an evolving and inclusive concept of citizenship. A balance was struck during the early post-war period between those two forces which shifted over time in favour of a gradual strengthening of the rights of a common citizenship over the privilege of class. The rapid widening of class differences has now thrown that movement into reverse, with the basis of class taking a dominant role over the idea of citizenship. Indeed, in the case of the most vulnerable, citizenship is in retreat. The means by which Mrs Thatcher has managed to put the 300-year development of citizenship into reverse is considered in Part II.

Part II

Mrs Thatcher's Class Strategy

During most of the post-war period, stubborn class differences in surviving birth, at school and with respect to income and health were the order of the day. While these class differences were sometimes wide, and while there is little to report on the lessening of such differences during the post-war period, the overall picture was at least one where class differences did not increase. Since 1979, however, a process of widening the class divisions in Britain has been set in motion, and this has played a part in expelling people from full citizenship. In this section, the various policies employed by the Government in its extension of this process are examined.

Widening the gap between social groups has always been part of Mrs Thatcher's philosophy. Soon after winning the leadership of the Conservative Party, she made plain her views on the sort of society she wished to help create in Britain. Speaking to an American audience, Mrs Thatcher expressed herself in the following terms:

Far more desirable and practicable than the pursuit of equality is the pursuit of equality of opportunity. Opportunity means nothing, unless it includes the right to be unequal – the freedom to be different. There is a saying in the mid-West of the United States of America: 'Don't cut down the tall poppies – let them rather grow tall'. I say: Let *our children* grow tall – and some grow taller than others if they have it in them to do so. (Margaret Thatcher, *Let Our Children Grow Tall*, Centre for Policy Studies, 1977, p. 12)

In Part I, an updating of Jan Pen's illustration of the unequal distribution of wealth was cited, where each of us is given a height corresponding to our income, so that we can take part in an hour-long procession (see pp. 28–30). Because of the large number of people on lowish incomes, those on average income do not appear until forty-five minutes have passed. Then the height of those in the procession increases rapidly, with the last minutes dominated by giants. Despite this very unequal distribution of income, Mrs Thatcher has reduced the 'height' of those at the beginning of the procession, while simultaneously adding generally to the 'height' of those who pass by in the last quarter of an hour, and particularly in the last minute, by enacting a series of interrelated initiatives, including a whole range of fiscal measures. The details of the distributional impact of each budget since 1979, which have been crucial in affecting the heights of those in the income procession, are given in the first part of this section. This is followed by a consideration of those measures that amount to an incomes policy against the poor. The range of reforms of the traditional welfare state, involving the cutting of benefits and disen-franchising people from benefit entitlement, is then considered. This is followed by details of how middle-class welfare has been provided, by means of a blank, signed cheque. The final topic considered is the likely effects of the poll tax, both in terms of income distribution and the rights to full citizenship of those who are unable to pay this new local government tax.

6

Incomes and Wealth Strategy

Since 1979, Mrs Thatcher has employed the full weight of fiscal policy, not only to halt the gentle trend towards greater equality in income that marked part of the post-war period, but actually to put the whole process into reverse. This has been perhaps one of the most breathtaking changes she has brought about over the past decade.

The main moves in this strategy have been initiated in the spring budgets. In the first budget after the 1979 election, the top rate of tax was reduced, from 83 to 60 per cent, and the widths of the remaining higher rate bands were extended. This budget set the trend for those that followed. The tax burden was cut by £4.5 billion. Of this total, the richest 1 per cent were awarded 15 per cent of the total tax cut. In the 1980 budget, and in all those from 1982 to 1985, the higher rate bands were indexed beyond the rate of inflation. The 1988 budget reduced the top rate of tax to 40 per cent.

Tall Parents

The Government is unwilling to part with information on the cumulative amount different income groups have gained from all the tax changes since 1979. What is available are figures on the amount different income groups have gained in any one tax year, as a result of tax changes in previous years, over and above the indexation that would have occurred. Had no additional budget changes been made to the tax regime of 1978–9, other than the indexation measures, then the overall level of taxation in 1988–9 would have been £20 billion higher in the current year. Of this sum, the richest 1 per cent of taxpayers would have paid an additional £4.7 billion in tax (23.5 per cent of the total). This group of 210,000 taxpayers has gained, on average, a tax reduction of £22,680 (*Hansard*, 14 July 1988, cols 319–20). Had no other tax changes occurred, other than indexation, the richest 10 per cent of taxpayers would have paid an additional tax bill amounting to £9.3 billion, or 46.5 per cent of the £20 billion total (*Hansard* 4 July 1988, cols 477–8). The bottom 50 per cent of taxpayers, numbering 10.5 million, would have paid an additional £3.4 billion in tax. This is equivalent to an average sum of £290 per taxpayer. Again, it must be stressed that these are not the cumulative gains of each group since 1979. These are the gains in the current year, taking into account the tax changes that have been brought about since 1979. Table 6.1 provides further details of the most significant redistribution of income to the rich since the dissolution of the monasteries.

Table 6.1 *Reduction in income tax in 1988 compared with 1978–1979 indexed regime (£ billion)*

Point of income distribution in 1988–9[a]	Numbers of units paying tax in 1988–9[b] millions	Total tax reduction £bn	Average reduction per taxpayer £
Top 1 per cent	0.21	4.70	22,380
Top 5 per cent	1.05	7.50	7,140
Top 10 per cent	2.10	9.30	4,430
Bottom 70 per cent[c]	14.70	6.20	420
Bottom 60 per cent[c]	12.60	4.70	370
Bottom 50 per cent[c]	10.50	3.40	320
Bottom 30 per cent[c]	6.30	1.50	240
Bottom 10 per cent[c]	2.10	0.40	190
All	20.90	20.00	960

[a] Based on 20,900,000 single people and married couples expected to pay tax in 1988–9, and excluding 1,100,000 who would pay tax under the revalorized 1978–9 regime.

[b] All information is in terms of tax units, i.e. married couples are counted as one and their incomes combined.

[c] Including reductions for those paying tax in 1988–9 and reductions for other units who would pay tax under the revalorized regime.

Source Hansard, 4 July 1988, cols 469–70.

With a redistribution on such an audacious scale, some of the Prime Minister's most ardent supporters have remained quiet about what has taken place. Others have gone onto the attack, defending the move on the ingenious grounds that the changes have resulted in the rich paying more tax. This argument has centred on the share of income tax paid by different income groups.

Despite the massive cuts in income tax, high-income earners have contributed an increasing proportion of the total tax 'take' since 1979. The top 1 per cent, for example, contributed 11.2 per cent of all income tax revenue in 1979–80, and 13.2 per cent by 1985–6. The figures for the top 5 per cent are 24 and 28.3 per cent (*Hansard*, 4 November 1988, cols 414–16). In commenting on these figures, the *Sunday Times* cited a *International Herald Tribune* editorial, which claimed that in Britain, as in America, cutting the top rates of tax has, in fact, increased the amount of tax paid by top earners. 'It has been proved', thundered Ferdinand Mount in the *Spectator*, 'that the effect of reducing penal top rates of taxation is that the Treasury receives more, not less revenue' (25 October 1986). Those who have benefited little if at all from the Tory's tax policies since 1979 are meant to draw a simple political conclusion: further cuts in the top rates of taxation will result in the rich paying even more tax.

The argument is not, however, as straightforward as some of the advocates would suggest. The reworked figures on a household basis, compiled by Michael O'Higgins and cited on pp. 53–5 are of relevance. These revealed that, since 1979, the share of income going to the richest group has substantially increased. With this group cornering a greater and greater share of the total largess, there should be little surprise that their share of the total tax take has also increased. But by how much has their share of income increased?

A recent Parliamentary Answer provided the following picture, although these data have not been reworked on a similar household basis. In the year before Mrs Thatcher's election, the top 1 per cent cornered 4.9 per cent of income before tax. By 1988–9, this had risen to 7.0 per cent (*Hansard*, 28 July 1988, cols 488–92). It is not surprising, therefore, that, even though this is a period of substantial reductions in the rate of tax, the richest income groups, which have gained a significantly increased proportion of the total pre-tax income, should consequently be contributing a greater proportion of the total tax take. However, and this is the crucial point consistently absent from justifications for the Thatcher changes, while the highest income groups are now contributing a greater share of the total tax take, their contribution in no way matches their increase in income. The share of tax paid by the top 1 per cent increased by a fairly modest 7.1 per cent while their share of income has jumped by 43 per cent.

Wealth Redistribution

Between 1925 and 1980, the data on wealth distribution reveal 'a strong underlying trend to less inequality' (T. Stark, *Income and Wealth in the 1980's*, Fabian Society, London, 1987, p. 10). On this front, the Government has almost certainly been successful in reversing what was a fifty-year trend – almost certainly, for the measures below detail the virtual disbandment of capital taxation, while the data for this period have yet to be published. Changes in the relative value of the different components of wealth – dwellings, land, stocks and shares – have played a part in ensuring that the wealthiest people have increased their share of wealth; so too has Government policy (see chapter 15 also for changes in the relative values of capital assets).

Major changes, affecting the position of the wealthiest groups, have been made by means of amendments to capital taxation. A minority of the very rich have a substantial income from wealth; in fact, only the very rich are in this position. Because this income gave rise to a further income without any actual work being performed, it attracted a special tax – the investment income surcharge. Immediately after assuming office, the Thatcher Government moved quickly to lower this tax on unearned income. In the 1979 budget, the threshold was doubled to £5,000. It was raised again to £5,500 in the following year, to £6,250 in 1982, and to £7,100 in 1983, before the charge on unearned income was abolished in 1984.

Major changes have also been made to capital transfer tax. The 1979 budget gave extended relief to discretionary trusts, which are one of the main means by which capital is kept intact but used for benefiting the families of the rich, and often the very rich. In the following budget, 1980, the nil rate band, exempting transfer from tax, was doubled to £50,000. In 1981, the Government introduced a lower lifetime rate, and increased annual exemptions from tax transferred to £3,000. The following three budgets, 1982, 1983 and 1984, saw further changes favouring those transferring capital, through changes in the rates of tax and changes to the rate bands. The 1985 budget raised further the exempt band from £64,000 to £67,000, while the budget of the following year abolished the tax altogether.

In its place, the Government claims to be introducing a new inheritance tax. The tax has, however, all the appearances of the old death duties tax, which essentially became a voluntary tax before it was abolished by the last Labour Government. Lifetime transfers have been made exempt. The ten-year accumulation period was reduced to seven years in the 1986 budget, while the exempt band was raised to £71,000. In the following year, this was raised to £90,000 and in 1988, raised again to £110,000, while the rates of tax were simplified into a single 40 per cent band.

The following changes have been made to the tax on capital gains. The threshold of gains in any one year was raised to £3,000 in 1980, and 'rollover' relief provisions were made for gifts. In 1982, the threshold was raised to £5,000, and the rollover relief was extended to trusts. In the following five budgets, from 1983 to 1987, the threshold was raised, up from £5,300 to £6,600 in 1987. In 1988, married couples became able to opt for taxation on an individual basis, and the tax threshold was reduced to £5,000. Two other changes were made that will have significant effects favouring the wealthy. All values for the tax were rebased to a March 1982 index, and the rate of tax was changed to equal the taxpayer's marginal rate.

There has been no study of the distributional impact of all these capital tax changes. Changes in capital gains tax alone have resulted in a current reduction in taxation of £1.2 billion, and because wealth is so unevenly distributed, this reduction has overwhelmingly benefited the very rich. Some idea of the total impact of the Government's changes in taxation on the transfer of wealth can be seen from information that the Government has released on the number of estates inherited free of tax. In 1978–9, twenty-three estates with net assets valued between £0.5 and £1 million were passed on free of inheritance tax. Eleven estates with net assets valued at over £1 million were also inherited without tax. The equivalent figures for 1985–6 were 152 and 53, respectively (*Hansard*, 13 July 1988, col. 198).

Summary

While the Government's privatization measures have gained considerable media coverage, and have been important in giving a large number of citizens their first stake in industrial capital, very little attention has been given to the almost revolutionary way Mrs Thatcher has redistributed other forms of income and wealth. This has been brought about by a whole series of budget changes that have been presented as 'tax cuts for all', but which have, in fact, redistributed income to those who are at the top end of the income scale – that is, those who pass by towards the very end of Pen's hour-long procession. Despite it being the Government's avowed intention to make Britain more unequal, the size of these gains has been so significant that the Government has refused to publish the cumulative gains of the very rich. The only information the Government is prepared to publish is the amount different income groups gained this year, as result of previous budget changes. These figures show that in 1988–9 the richest 1 per cent – or 210,000 taxpayers – cornered £4.7 billion in tax cuts. Individually, this works out at £22,680 reduction in tax for each of these taxpayers. Just how significant this sum is becomes apparent when it is recalled that this increase in income by way of tax reductions is greater than the *total* income of any single person in the bottom 95 per cent of the population. Similarly, the Government has moved quickly to reduce the tax on capital. The tax on unearned income has been abolished, the effect of the capital gains tax much reduced, while the tax on the transfer of cpaital has been abolished and replaced by an even more modest inheritance tax. Each of these moves helps to explain the widening dispersion of post-tax income and wealth that was commented on in Part I. This policy has also played a prominent part in isolating the most vulnerable group at the bottom of the income pile.

7

Incomes Policy for Poverty

At the same time as using the fiscal system to reroute income to the wealthy, the Government has pursued a policy of reducing the relative pay of many low-paid workers. The stated belief is that lower pay will result in increased employment, and the Government has pursued its goal of reducing the rewards to the lowest paid by co-ordinating five different policies: the abolition of the Fair Wages Resolution; the abolition of the 'Schedule 11' procedure; the dismantling of part of the Wages Council machinery; the subsidizing of employers who offer jobs at low rates of pay; and, finally, through a more general campaign designed to 'talk down' wages.

Fair Wages Resolution

The history of the Fair Wages Resolution goes back to 1891, when the House of Commons gave its unanimous approval to a resolution aimed at ensuring that employers tendering for public contracts should pay the wages generally accepted in the trade for similar work. During the past hundred years, this protective machinery was extended to different parts of the labour market. The earlier reforms centred on extending the remit of the resolution within the public sector, but during World War Two the procedure was extended to the private sector.

In July 1982, the Government announced its intention to rescind the Fair Wages Resolution. In so doing, it marshalled a number of arguments to make its case, only two of which are of direct relevance here. In the first place, the Government stressed that the Resolution was inconsistent with its belief that pay and conditions should be determined by employers and unions, according to the pressures of the market. This first argument is a clear statement of Government belief, and can only be challenged by those who hold a different approach to the role of government in general, and the full range of forces that operate when determining wage levels in particular.

The Government's second justification for its actions can be challenged on the grounds of factual accuracy. In a letter to employers, the Government argued that the Resolution was out of date, as: 'Collective bargaining arrangements have increased to the extent where the great majority of employees have their pay and conditions of employment determined by agreed, voluntary arrangements in the light of the particular circumstances of the parties concerned' (letter dated 25 May 1982).

The latest available information on trade union membership does not, however, substantiate the Government's claim. The figures reveal that in 1980 union membership fell by 3.7 per cent, from a post-war peak of 13,289,000. This trend continued into 1985, with a fall to 10,716,000. A similar decline, though less marked, is evident from an examination of the rate of union density, which is gauged by dividing the potential union membership by the actual membership. In 1979, union density stood at 55.4 per cent. It fell the following year to 53.6 per cent, and again, in 1986, to 49 per cent.

The Employment Secretary might try to use these figures to support his claim that 'the great majority of employees' have their pay and conditions determined by collective agreements. In his favour is the fact that many non-trade unionists work in establishments where pay is determined by the efforts of their trade union colleagues. But his assertion has less validity once the level of unionization in the private sector, where the vast majority of Government contracts are placed, is taken into consideration. Two areas that can be expected to gain a greater number of Government contracts as the privatization of public services continues are the construction industry and those activities classified as private services. Union membership in the latter category stands at less than 20 per cent, whereas in the construction industry it has fallen over recent years, to 36.7 per cent by 1979. Moreover, not all union members have had their pay set by collective agreements. While union membership stood at around 12 million in 1982, the Government estimates that only 10.7 million manual workers are covered by collective agreements and statutory wage orders (*Hansard*, 25 July 1983, cols 322–3). By 1987, the number of manual workers covered by collective agreements and statutory wage orders had fallen to an estimated 6.6 million (*Hansard*, 25 July 1988, col. 174). In September 1983, the Fair Wages Resolution ceased to have any effect on protecting the pay and conditions of Britain's low-paid workers.

Schedule 11

Early in the 1979 Parliament, the Government made plain its intention to scrap the Schedule 11 protection offered to low-paid workers. In doing so, the Government advanced the following justification. Ministers asserted that the main objective of Schedule 11 was to be the abolition of 'pockets of low pay' that exist in all industries, including those known to pay higher than average wages. However, action had not been confined to workers on low pay, as 'many higher paid groups ... benefited from [Schedule 11] awards'. Again, the accuracy of the Government's contention can be challenged.

The Industrial Relations Research Unit at the University of Warwick examined the claims made under the Schedule 11 procedure for the period 1977–9. In 1977, the Unit's analysis of successful claims showed that ninety-seven were on behalf of manual workers earning less than median earnings, and only twenty-one came from manual workers earning more than this level. The equivalent figures for non-manual workers were, respectively, ninety-six and four.

The data for 1979 show an even greater number of successful claims being made on behalf of workers earning less than median earnings. Of the successful claims for manual workers, 93 per cent were on behalf of workers earning less than the average, and only 7 per cent for those earning above this level. For non-manual workers, the picture was, respectively, 87 and 13 per cent. The protection afforded by Schedule 11 was abolished in 1980.

Dismantling the Wages Councils

Wages Councils have their roots in what were originally called 'Trades Boards', the first four of which were established by the Trades Boards Act in 1909. The system was extended after World War One, and they were renamed Wages Councils at the end of World War Two. Despite the fact that these councils have the power to lay down minimum rates of remuneration, many workers covered by the Wages Council machinery remain low paid. While something like 25 per cent of all workers are low paid (defined here for the sake of illustration as less than two-thirds of average earnings), a little over 70 per cent of all Wages Council employees are so categorized, despite the fact that the Wages Council sector employs less than 14 per cent of all employees. And yet it is this sector, employing a disproportionate number of low-paid individuals, that has been singled out for a two-pronged Government campaign aimed at reducing the level of wage settlements.

The first part of the campaign on the level of wages set by Wages Councils has been conducted in the House of Commons, by ministers expressing unease at the level of wage settlements agreed by different Wages Councils, and particularly at the rates paid to young workers. On one occasion, when the Employment Secretary was asked whether the level of settlements in the Wages Council sector was preventing employers from recruiting more workers, he replied:

It is self-evident that wages are ultimately limited by the ability of employers to pay, which is, in turn, limited by the prices which, in the light of home and overseas competition, they are able to [charge] for their products. There is, therefore, little doubt that the higher the level at which councils set minimum wages, the fewer people will be employed.   (*Hansard*, 6 July 1982, col. 139 oral)

The questioner had asked the Employment Secretary if he would commission a survey to investigate the effect of Wages Council settlements on employment levels. He replied: 'I am doubtful that a survey could readily quantify this effect, i.e. the effect on unemployment levels' (*Hansard*, 6 July 1982, col. 139 oral).

While ministers have remained unwilling to test their theories in the market place by conducting research to see whether the Wage Council settlements have resulted in lost jobs, they nevertheless concurrently conducted a private correspondence with the Council chairmen expressing public concern about the level of settlements. Since 1979, the Government has written directly to Wages Councils on five separate occasions. Each of these missives has attempted to persuade the chairman and independent members of the Council concerned (who have the casting votes when employers and employee representatives disagree) to make awards lower than they might otherwise do. By

1984 this softly-softly approach gave way to a more direct intervention.

Direct intervention came by way of a reform of the Wages Council machinery. The 1986 Wages Council Act has brought about three major changes. First, it excludes workers aged under twenty-one, of whom there are approximately 500,000, from the protection of a minimum wage offered by the Wages Council procedure. The Government believes that such exclusion will encourage the creation of new jobs by ensuring that: 'an employer is not prevented from employing young people at wages they are prepared to accept, because the rates are below those set by the Wages Councils' (Department of Employment Press Notice, 26 July 1986).

Second, for the workers who are still covered, it effectively limited the power of Wage Councils, by allowing them to set only one basic hourly rate of pay, an overtime rate and a limit on charges for any accommodation provided by the employer. Wages Councils have also been instructed to consider the impact on jobs of the minimum rates of pay that they impose. Further, Wages Councils are no longer able to set holiday entitlements, weekend pay, shift premiums, guarantee pay or skill differentials. Third, the 1986 Wages Council Act has simplified the procedure for reviewing the scope of Wages Councils, or even for abolishing them.

These changes have had their intended effect on wage rates. In clothing, the minimum rate for adult workers in 1988 stood at £77.54 for a 39-hour week – or £1.99 per hour. In other Wages Councils, the minimum rates tended to converge around £2–2.30 per hour. The average hourly wage in the rest of the economy was £5.35 an hour. The Low Pay Unit points to the 'most damning indictment' of the rates set by the Wages Councils as being 'their failure even to guarantee an income above the poverty line' (*The Great Pay Robbery*, LPU, 1988, p. 11)

[A]n hourly rate of £2.16 would be needed just to provide a single person, after a full week's work, with an income equivalent to that which they would receive if unemployed and dependent on income support. Most wages councils establish rates which are lower than this, or very little higher. . . . Of the main wages councils, only those covering the retail trade exceed the poverty line for a single person, and even then by a margin of only 17p an hour. In all the other main wages council sectors, the minimum rates stand at or below the level of subsistence. Moreover, these comparisons are based on a single person living alone. No assumptions about dependants have been used. The poverty line for anyone with children or other dependants is much higher.   (pp. 11–12)

Subsidies to Low-paid Jobs

At a time when the machinery that provided a floor to the setting of
wage rates was being abolished, the Government was also laying plans
encouraging employers to take on workers at low rates of pay. The
Jobstart allowance was initially run on a pilot basis in nine areas, before
being made nationwide in 1986. The aim of the allowance is to offer a
financial incentive to the long-term unemployed in order to encourage
them back into work. From July 1986, everyone aged eighteen and
over, who has more than six months to go before reaching the state
retirement age, and who has been out of work for more than twelve
months, is eligible for the Jobstart allowance. The one remaining
stipulation is that their new employment offers gross earnings of less
than £80 a week. Since the inception of the scheme, the Government
has paid out 24,000 allowances to workers earning less than this sum.

In March 1986, the Government announced a second scheme to
subsidize low-paid employment. Called the New Workers' Scheme
(NWS), it replaced what was called the Young Workers' Scheme. The
Government offers a subsidy of £15 a week to employers, excluding
those in the public services or domestic households, who recruit
eighteen and nineteen year olds in their first year of employment at
wages below £55 a week. Payments apply to full-time jobs and last for
one year. According to the Department of Employment, the scheme is
designed to boost the employment prospects of those who have just
left, or who are too old for the Youth Training Scheme.

How true is it that the scheme will provide an incentive for
employers to create jobs? A survey of the Young Workers' Scheme
('Evaluation of the Young Worker's Scheme', *Employment Gazette*,
May 1986) shows the effect of the scheme on pay levels, noting that:

between February and December 1984, the average YWS wage was
£40 a week;

employers reported that this was £2.40 a week less than they would
have paid in the absence of the scheme, which, therefore, constitutes a
wage cut of 6 per cent;

employers were able to cut wages more substantially where a YWS job
was substituting for another. Employers reported average savings of
around £20 a week.

This small survey has the advantage of indicating just how large a subsidy – in the form of Government grants and wage reductions – employers have gained under the two schemes. Some employers have gained job subsidies of around £17.40 a week (the £15 government subsidy, plus an average pay cut of £2.40 a week), while others have marked up savings of around £35 a week per job, derived from a £20 a week pay cut, plus the £15 government subsidy. Again, the numbers 'benefiting' from the scheme are revealing. From the inception of the scheme until its closure on January 1988, almost 59,000 applications were approved.

Summary

To match the redistribution brought about by successive tax changes since 1979, which have benefited the very rich on a scale undreamed of, the Government has been pursuing a co-ordinated attack on the wage levels of those earning least on the grounds that high money wage rates – at least for those at the bottom of the income pile – prevent considerable numbers of people from obtaining employment. It has therefore embarked on a policy of reducing the wages paid in Britain's lowest paid trades. The minimum underpinning given by the Fair Wages Resolution and Schedule 11 has been scrapped. Similarly, the simplification of the powers of the Wages Council system has resulted in the exemption of young workers from the statutory entitlement to a minimum wage. So as to combat what commentators on high pay call the 'stickiness' of wage rates, which prevents them adapting to market conditions at the bottom end of the income scale, the Government offers subsidies to employers, providing they take on young workers earning less then £55 per week. All these moves have played a part in the record fall in the relative pay of Britain's lowest paid workers – to the lowest on record – and helps to explain the grounds for the decisive shift in the distribution of pre-tax income, which was detailed in chapter 6. This shift in income provides another part of the answer to the question of why it is that Britain, which has never been materially richer as a country, should be witnessing the birth of an underclass, whose living standards, social standing, life chances, hopes and aspirations cut them off from the rest of Britain. Welfare changes have also been made to reinforce this trend towards greater inequality, and, equally importantly, to disenfranchising large numbers of people from non-means-tested benefits.

8

Welfare Strategies

The third part of Mrs Thatcher's strategy of creating an enterprise culture, which massively rewards those at the top while penalizing those at the bottom of the income pile, has been the launching of a series of reforms of the welfare state. This strategy has at different points in time involved the abolition of certain benefits, a reduction in the numbers eligible to those that remain, the curtailment of the rate of increase in the value of benefits and real cuts in their financial worth. This chapter looks at how each of the different aspects of this strategy has been employed, not only to free money from welfare for tax cuts but also to gain an appreciation of the extent of the disenfranchisement from an insurance-based welfare that has occurred. The 'cost' of the Government's overall strategy of creating an incentive-based society has been high – quite apart from the hardship caused to the millions of individuals affected. Cutting the value of, or abolishing national insurance benefits, and a much increased reliance on means-tested assistance, has played a crucial part in trapping the underclass into long-term dependency, although such an outcome is in stark contradiction to the Government's stated long-term objectives.

Uprating Formula

The most significant welfare change, both in terms of numbers of people affected and the sum saved in public expenditure, has been the method by which this Government has calculated increases in social security. The 1974 Labour Government insisted that what are known as long-term benefits, such as old-age pensions and invalidity benefit, should increase in line with prices or earnings, whichever was the more advantageous for the claimants. This dual safeguard, which was designed not merely to maintain the real value of benefits, but also to guarantee that they paralleled any increase in the real incomes of the working population, was removed in 1980. Since then, the Government has had a statutory responsibility to increase benefits only in line with prices. Had the previous policy been continued, the single pension would now be £9.80 in excess of what has, in fact, been paid since April 1988. For a married couple, the loss on the weekly pension amounts to £15.70. The most obvious result of such 'cuts' has been to affect most adversely those without any other pension provision, and has led to an increase in the numbers claiming means-tested support. The effect of this on the Government's aim of making more people independent of the state, as well as the effect on increasing disincentives, is considered in Part III.

Earnings-related Supplements

The second major change to the welfare state that has taken place since 1979 has been the abolition of the earnings-related supplements (ERS). In 1968, the Labour Government introduced a series of earnings-related supplements which were paid on top of the existing flat-rate national insurance benefits of unemployment pay, sick pay, industrial injury benefit, maternity and widow's allowances. Those supplements were reduced in January 1981, and finally abolished a year later, in January 1982. There was, however, no concomitant reduction in each worker's contribution to the National Insurance Fund. The working population has thus continued to make contributions for which they gain no benefit.

The estimated average ERS paid along with unemployment benefit in 1981 was £8.00, with an upper limit of £14.00. Had the changes brought about by the 1980 Social Security Act not taken place, the maximum payment in 1981 would have been £19.25. Had the supplements still been in existence, they would, of course, have been reviewed each year. The Government estimates that a third of the savings in public expenditure created by the abolition of these supplements was lost in a resulting increase in supplementary benefit payments. This is another say of indicating the number forced to resort to means-tested assistance as a result of the abolition of their earnings-related benefits.

Phasing-out of Child Additions

The third change, or cut in welfare provision since 1979 has been the
phasing-out of the child additions, which were paid to claimants of
national insurance unemployment and sick pay, and the significant
reduction in the value of the additions paid to other insurance benefits.
This reduction was achieved by a change in the calculation of the
uprating of these additions. The intricacies of the alteration itself,
begun in 1980, are not directly relevant here. What is of concern is the
size and impact of this reduction. This change had by the November
1983 uprating resulted in the abolition of short-term child support.

Child Benefits

The fourth of the welfare alterations centres on the child benefit
scheme. This benefit, phased in over a number of years, came fully
into operation in 1979, and replaced child tax allowances and family
allowances. The value of the new benefit was significantly enhanced by
an additional £1.5 billion of revenue that was pumped into the scheme
at the time.

Over the past eight years, Conservative ministers have projected an
image of themselves as the party of the family. Since 1979, however,
their record has not always conformed to this declared objective. Child
benefit, the principal family benefit, has not been increased in line with
pensions and other benefits. In the Government's first review of social
security benefits in 1979, pensions were increased by 19.5 per cent, in
line with price rises, but there was no increase whatsoever in child
benefit. This omission was offset in November 1983 by an increase of
a little over 11 per cent, while pensions and other benefits increased by
3.7 per cent. However, the November 1985 review saw a return to a
policy of discriminating against child benefit. Long-term benefits such
as pensions were increased by 7 per cent, whereas child benefit was
increased by a mere 2.2 per cent. In the November review of both
1987 and 1988, the Government announced the freezing of child
benefit payments since the 1988 statement there have been numerous
ominous statements, all stressing that the future of the benefit is
'under review'.

Benefits into Tax

Under the National Insurance Act of 1945, all welfare benefits were made taxable. This position remained unchanged until 1949 when, for reasons of administrative convenience to the Inland Revenue, short-term benefits were excluded from tax liability. In the 1980 budget, the Government announced that unemployment pay, sickness and invalidity benefit would be liable to tax. The primary reason for this move was not a desire for increased tax revenue, welcome as this no doubt was, but, rather, an expression of the Government's opposition to people enjoying a larger income when out of work than they could take home in a wage packet. Moreover, the Government proposed different ways whereby these three benefits could be made liable to tax.

The most novel approach related to sickness benefit. It was decided that state sickness benefit was to be taxed by its abolition! From April 1983, the first eight weeks of sickness benefit were to be met by the employer. While many workers continued to enjoy full pay, at least in the initial stages of illness, others were less fortunate, and gained only the statutory minimum. Whichever option was adopted, employers include sickness benefit as part of their employee's taxable income. Since April 1986, the whole of the twenty-eight weeks of sickness benefit has been the responsibility of employers, and all twenty-eight weeks is taxable. The benefit currently paid is below what would have been the level of state sickness benefit.

The Government initially laid down three rates of sickness benefit, covering those on very low, low and modest earnings. In 1986, this structure was altered by a merging of the middle and lower rates. Those who previously qualified for the former, therefore, have lost out substantially, as their sickness pay has been cut by almost 20 per cent. The DSS estimates that around 5.5 million people each year receive statutory sick pay, and that 15 per cent of this total belonged to the bottom and middle earnings bands. Almost half a million workers will, therefore, be adversely affected annually by the Government's 'simplification'. Hardest hit are those on lowest incomes, as employers are allowed to pay them at a specially designed low rate.

The Government discovered an equally ingenious way of taxing invalidity benefit. When announcing the increase in such benefits for 1981, it disclosed its intention to increase invalidity benefit by 5 per cent less than the rise in prices. This reduction, or, as the Government preferred to call it, abatement, was in lieu of taxation. For good measure, the Government also announced that, while waiting to introduce the statutory sick pay scheme, sickness benefit would be similarly 'abated', as would unemployment benefit. A year later, the Government restored the 5 per cent abatement in that year's uprating of benefits, conceding that it was experiencing considerable difficulties in making invalidity benefit liable to taxation by the following year.

Initially, the Government accepted that the 5 per cent abatement would also be lifted from other short-term benefits when these became taxable. The Government did not honour this commitment when unemployment benefit became taxable in July 1982. According to the new rules, eligible claimants continue to draw benefit, from which no deduction of tax is made. At the end of a period of unemployment, however, the unemployment benefit office notifies the claimant of the amount of taxable benefit that has been paid to them. This sum is then included as part of a claimant's taxable income during the relevant tax year. Similarly, those unemployed claimants drawing income support have found that their benefit, up to the standard rate of unemployment benefit, is liable to taxation. The revenue derived from taxing unemployment benefit, and the relevant part of an unemployed claimant's supplementary benefit stood at an estimated £600 million in 1985–6.

Housing Benefit Scheme

Changes in the value of housing benefit constitute the sixth reform of welfare since 1979. In fact, the housing benefit scheme only came fully into operation in April 1983. The scheme replaced the rent allowance and rebate scheme, the rate rebate scheme, and the payment of rent to supplementary benefit claimants. The scheme does not cover owner-occupiers who require assistance with mortgage interest payments, or boarders requiring help with their board and lodging charges, although the Government has given notice that it intends to review these payments. Both of these categories may be helped under the income support scheme. In 1984–5, over 7 million households, or one in three of all households, were in receipt of housing benefit, and the cost was equal to more than 10 per cent of the entire social security budget.

There has been a whole series of changes to the scheme since its introduction in April 1983, with additional reforms a likely prospect. Many of these changes have centred on what are called tapers. Where a claimant's income rises above the 'needs allowance', tapers are applied so that, as income rises, the size of benefit falls in direct relation to the excess income over the needs allowance. A similar process operates in reverse for those with incomes below the needs allowance.

By 1988, the Government had already made five changes to the tapers, each of which reduced the amount of benefit paid to those whose incomes are above the needs allowance level. A further major 'saving' in the scheme has been achieved by increasing the contributions that non-dependants are expected to make towards their housing costs. The total cuts in housing benefit deriving from such changes have reduced the projected expenditure by £950 million.

In February 1984, the Housing Benefit Review was established by the Government which, subsequent to receiving the Review's report, published a Green Paper detailing a series of reforms (*Reform of Social Security*, Cmnd. 9518, HMSO, 1985). Some of the reforms are eminently sensible and have been introduced. The suggestion of a common income test, based on net income, with incomes below the suggested new income support level gaining full relief with rent is a welcome change. But accompanying this reform, which was aimed at lessening the disincentive effect of moving from benefit to work, are provisos like the requirement that recipients of housing benefit will be expected to meet 20 per cent of their rates bill which are cuts in welfare payments. Other proposed changes included the simplification of the various existing tapers by creating a single taper, which withdraws housing support from those whose incomes are above the income support level at a faster rate than before. These changes have all been implemented, and have resulted in a reduction of housing costs on what was the projected level by £450 million in 1988–9.

Latest Changes

Supplementary Benefit was replaced by income support in 1988. Under the old system, a person was eligible for supplementary benefit if their resources were below their requirements. The requirements were approved annually by Parliament, and were determined by a scale rate of benefit, together with a whole series of regular weekly additions. As was seen in Part I, while some claimants would qualify for the ordinary rate of benefit, others would be eligible for the long-term rate, which for a married couple was valued at 25 per cent higher than the ordinary rate. All other claimants under pensionable age – except the unemployed – qualified for the long-term rate after being on benefit for a year. In addition, some claimants of both the ordinary and the long-term rates were awarded weekly additions to meet special needs such as extra heating, diet or laundry costs. There were also additions to cover housing costs such as water rates, and owner-occupiers received help with mortgage interest, and an allowance towards insurance and repairs. Tenants on supplementary benefit automatically received 100 per cent rent rebates, and both owner-occupiers and tenants received payments to cover their rates in full. As mentioned above, against these requirements would be put a claimant's resources, and a person became eligible for supplementary benefit if their resources were less than their requirements, the difference between the two being the sum paid in Supplementary Benefit.

Under the income support system, if a person's resources are less than what is deemed to be his or her 'applicable amount' of Income Support, then eligibility is gained. However, the applicable amount does not make a distinction between those eligible for a long-term as opposed to an ordinary rate, nor is there a distinction between a householder and non-householder, although there are additions for special needs. Under the income support system, as opposed to housing benefit, the only major housing costs that will be met in part or in full will be mortgage interest. Housing costs will only be covered if claimants are eligible for housing benefit. A claimant's rates bills will not be met in full; only 80 per cent of this sum will be covered by housing benefit. The Government claims that income support rates have been increased by an amount to cover what on average is the 20 per cent rate bill for the entire country. This sum is £1.30; in Birkenhead only 272 tenants pay less than this sum on a 20 per cent contribution. In contrast, 1,100 tenants are being asked to pay more than £2.40 as their 20 per cent contribution.

The Government's claim that the new income support scheme is more generous than the now-defunct supplementary benefit system will be considered below. It is important to stress how these changes – whatever their merits – have played a structural role in helping sustain an underclass. Their role has been structural in the sense that it is the social security rules, rather than personal failure or character defect, that are the relevant factor to be considered. The group that has been most adversely affected under the new scheme is the unemployed under the age of twenty-five. Under the supplementary benefit scheme, many of this group would have qualified for the householder rate – valued at £30.40. Under the new scheme this group of claimants gain a weekly benefit valued at £27.40 but from this the claimant has to pay both 20 per cent of his or her rates bill and, similarly, 20 per cent of the water rates bill.

At the same time as introducing the new income support scheme, the rules for eligibility to housing benefit have been tightened. Claimants with capital below £3,000 will have this sum ignored, whereas those with capital in excess of £8,000 will find themselves ineligible for benefit. A weekly tariff income is used to make deductions from income support for capital between these two sums. If income is at or below the applicable amount (the eligibility rates for income support) the maximum rebate will be paid, which is 100 per cent for rent and 80 per cent for rates. If a person's income is above the applicable amount, these rebates will be reduced, producing a loss of 65 per cent of the difference between their income and the applicable amount for rent, and suffering a 20 per cent tapered reduction for rates. In total the withdrawal rate for some claimants with incomes above the applicable amount is over 80 per cent.

The significance of these changes can be seen from the numbers disqualified from benefit and the total saving in public expenditure. A House of Commons Library reference note on the latest housing benefit changes points out that these cuts alone will result in an annual saving of £1.8 billion (*Public Expenditure White Paper*, Cmnd. 228 – II, table 15.6), while reducing by about a million the number of people eligible for housing benefit.

What then of the Government's claim that it is spending more money in income support than it would have done had the previous supplementary benefit system remained in place? It is impossible to check the validity of this statement, as the Government has consistently refused to provide the key information necessary to make this calculation, namely details on what would have paid out in the uprating allowance of supplementary benefit had it still been in force in April 1988. Not surprisingly, therefore, the Government's claims regarding who is better off have become an issue of intense dispute. Because income support was introduced at a time when there would otherwise have been an increase in supplementary benefits, and because transitional protection has been provided for some groups of claimants who have been transferred to income support, the Government claims that relatively few people suffered an actual cut in benefit in April 1988. But how is 'relatively few' defined? On the Government's own figures this total is almost a million people – 960,000 in fact. However, as Julia Lourie points out in a House of Commons Brief:

the structural reform will create 3,650,000 losers (i.e. their income will be lower than it would have been if the old system had continued and been up-rated in the normal way, and there had been no transitional protection) compared with 3,190,000 gainers (the Government claims that 5,000,070 gained) while 1,680,000 people remain unaffected. (*Social Security Changes*, April 1988, House of Commons Library Research Note 385, 1988, p. 10)

Since these calculations were made the government has raised the capital level for those qualifying for housing benefit.

Summary

While the reform of the welfare state has not attracted the same consistent media attention as other issues, the changes made in the scope of welfare provision since 1979 nevertheless amount to a mini-revolution, and have played a part in creating an underclass. The Government's overall aim has been threefold. The first has been to reduce the rate at which welfare expenditure was increasing. Since 1979, cuts on the national insurance benefits, such as old-age pensions and unemployment pay have resulted in savings in excess of £15 billion. Currently, the annual saving is in the region of £5 billion, only slightly more than the sum that the Government gave away in tax cuts to the richest 1 per cent of taxpayers in the 1988 budget. The second aim has been to reduce the attractiveness and the scope of the welfare state, in order that people begin seeking private or company provision. An important side-effect of both these objectives has been the significant increase in the numbers caught in the dependency culture of means-tested assistance. Denying entitlement to whole groups of the population has been the third aim, and this has been particularly noticeable in the case of young claimants. While these changes do not alone amount to a decisive shift in the social and political culture, they none the less have a crucial role in shaping people's feelings about themselves and their own worth. Means-tested assistance is equated by the customer with second-class citizenship. Moreover, the severity of the treatment meted out to this underclass, who have borne the brunt of the welfare changes, is in stark contrast to the benevolent attitude demonstrated by the Government in its welfare policies for the most privileged. The system of tax welfare is considered in chapter 10.

9

Poll Tax

Local government services are currently financed from three sources: rates on domestic property; rates on business property; and a revenue support grant from central government. From 1990 local government services will still be financed from three sources, but the nature of the funding will be radically different. Domestic rates will be abolished and in their place local authorities will levy a poll tax. Whereas rates were levied on property, the poll tax will be levied on individuals. Whereas rates were indirectly related to income, or at least past income (in that they were proportional to the value of the home in which people lived), the poll tax will take no account of the financial circumstances on whom the tax is levied. A central government grant will continue to be paid to local authorities. A business rate will also be levied, but both these two components of local authority finance will be radically restructured.

Limiting Local Funding

The Government has three objectives in mind in its near-revolutionary reform of local government finance. It is determined that local businesses, who have no direct vote to the local authority, unless the owners live within the same district as their firms, should not be driven out of inner-city areas by an ever-escalating rates bill. Hence the Government will set a national business rate. Once this rate has been set, the only revision allowed will be to keep its value in line with inflation. There is no possibility, therefore, of local authorities being able to increase the size of the business rate in an attempt to finance an expansion of local services.

Nor will the second element in the new system of local government support – the central government grant – be open to a similar revision. Previously the support from central government was to some extent related to the provision of services, which were themselves related to local needs, at least in the view of the local authority. The Government now intends to draw up its own inventory of local needs and set a contribution to the local authority that will allow for the provision of those minimum needs in year one. Changes in the level of support in future years will only be made to take account of inflation or changes in the size and composition of the total population within each local authority area. There is to be no discussion with local authorities on how this needs index is drawn up, and there will be no appeal against the size of the government grant that results from using this calculation. As one of the aims of the reform of local government is to impose a ceiling on local authority expenditure, it is unlikely that the formula drawn up by the Government will allow a generous provision of local services.

The only flexibility in a local authority's ability to raise finance will be the poll tax, which on current reckoning is intended to make up only 20 per cent of a local authority's revenue base. Raising additional funds on this narrow tax base will mean very significant increases in the tax. Those authorities most likely to be in need of raising additional finance will be those with large numbers of people on low incomes living within their boundaries. Yet it will be those on low incomes who will be most affected by any additional increases in the size of the poll tax. The Government's reform of local authority finance is therefore likely to lead to a deterioration in local authority services, be they health, education or welfare. And because these services play a more important part in the lives of people on low than on higher incomes, the move is likely to reduce still further the relative living standards of the poor, and particularly the most vulnerable in the underclass.

Redistribution

The poll tax will bring about a significant redistribution of income between different households and individuals within those households. In presenting who gains and loses, the Government has been careful to cite figures based on the number of households. It claims that whereas 7.9 million households will be losers under the poll tax, there will be

11.1 million households who gain – in other words, pay less in poll tax than they do currently in rates. Overwhelmingly those who gain live in small households, and particularly single-person households: 2.5 million single-pensioner households will gain, whereas the Government estimates less than a half a million losers amongst this group. In contrast, of households with three or more adults only half a million will be gainers, whereas 1.5 million will be losers. The picture changes dramatically, however, if adults rather than households are used as the basis of the calculation. While 18.3 million adults are shown on the Government's figures to be gainers, 17 million are shown to be losers. These losers are heavily concentrated in two-pensioner households and other households with two or more adults.

The Government data show that the numbers of gainers and losers also varies in different parts of the country. In the South-East (excluding London) – one of the richest areas of the kingdom – Government data show that 73 per cent of households will be gainers under the new tax. In contrast, in the North, 61 per cent of households will be asked to pay more towards local government services.

All the Government data are based on 'averages', which do not give an accurate picture of the effects of a poll tax, either on local authorities or on individuals within those local authorities. A number of local studies have been undertaken on what the impact of the poll tax would be had it been implemented in the 1988–9 financial year. Some of these surveys, for example the one carried out in Birmingham, illustrate the different impact of the tax if individuals rather than households are chosen as the basis for the calculation. Whereas a majority, 54 per cent, of households in Birmingham would have gained under the poll tax if it had been levied in 1988–9, only 39 per cent of adults are shown to be gainers. A very similar picture emerges in Haringey, but here the local authority has worked out the numbers whose income will be affected by more than £2 a week. In the 1988–9 financial year, the poll tax would have resulted in 53 per cent of households paying less tax in Haringey than under the old rating system. However, on the basis of individuals, the numbers of gainers falls to 36.5 per cent. But of the winners only 2 per cent are shown to be better off by £2 a week, whereas 39 per cent of losers will be asked to pay a local poll tax that is more than £2 above their then current rate contribution (*Poll Tax Facts*, no. 9, Local Government Information Unit, 1988).

The Government claims that the poor will be protected from finding themselves amongst this group of losers by the national system of rebates that will operate alongside the new scheme. The Government made clear when introducing its reform of the housing benefit scheme in April 1988 that it will be adapted to provide community charge rebates for low-income groups. The rebates will operate in a similar way to rate rebates, and will be administered by local authorities as part of the housing benefit scheme. As with rates, the rebates will be available for up to only 80 per cent of the community charge. As with the present system, there will be help for those who receive the full rebates: additional payments are to be made to Income Support rates to cover the 20 per cent minimum community charge.

One group on low income who will lose out consists of those people living in areas where the poll tax is levied at a higher rate than the Government calculates, and who in consequence will have to meet a 20 per cent poll tax bill that is larger than that calculated by the 20 per cent met by the Government. Another group who will lose out will be those on low incomes who are ineligible for income support but qualify for housing benefit. This group will have 80 per cent of their poll tax met but will be required to meet 20 per cent of the tax from their own income. A further group will also lose, despite the existence of a rebate scheme. Under the current system the Government calculates that large numbers of those eligible for housing benefit do not claim. The latest official figures were for 1984 when about one in four eligible claimants failed to register for a rebate.

Loss of Citizenship

Each local authority must compile a register containing the names and addresses of those within the area who are liable to pay the tax and the dates from which they become, or cease to be, liable. The first register has to be completed by 1 December 1989. Its compilation will probably run in tandem with work on the 1989–90 electoral register. Chief finance officers of district councils, London boroughs and the Isles of Scilly and the City of London have been designated as 'Community Charge Registration Officers' for their area. These officers have the power to inspect the electoral registration register, and electoral registration officers have a similar power to compare names on their list with those that may or may not be appearing on the poll tax register. The Government has ensured, therefore, that if a

person enters his or her name on the register in order to vote, he or she
will also be billed for the poll tax.

One way of making it more difficult for the Community Charge
Registration Officers to trace people will be if they disappear from the
electoral register. Avoiding the poll tax will be costly in terms of
universal political citizenship. The group most likely to opt for
non-registration will be the very poorest, and particularly those in the
underclass. While other economic and social changes are undermining
full economic and social citizenship for the underclass, any retreat
from universal political citizenship results in the underclass losing the
little political clout they have to reverse this trend.

Summary

The introduction of the poll tax will doubly exacerbate those forces
that are giving rise to an underclass in Britain. The tax will shift the
burden of local taxation between different households and different
income groups. The Government's claim that those on low incomes
will be better off under the new scheme, or at least see their financial
position protected, is unlikely to be borne out by events. A number of
those on income support will find that the compensatory payments to
cover their 20 per cent poll tax contribution will be less than the actual
contribution they have to make. Similarly, those who are in work and
on low income, or who for other reasons are ineligible for income
support, may be eligible for the equivalent of a rate rebate under the
existing system. Under the scheme as it was originally cast, let alone
before the Government began reducing both the numbers eligible and
the value of the benefit paid, many low-income poll tax payers would
have found themselves making a substantial contribution after receiving whatever the rebate to which they are entitled. A third group will
similarly lose out under the poll tax proposals: one in four of those
currently eligible for housing benefit do not claim. This group will
have to meet its poll tax contribution in full. The one redress any of the
members of this group have is to try not to appear on the poll tax
register. Given the link the Government has forged between the
collection of data for the local tax and the registration of the very same
individuals for the vote, the cost of non-payment will be the loss of the
remaining political clout the underclass has with which to fight its way
back into mainstream Britain.

10

Boosting Middle-class Welfare

Much of the Government-initiated debate on welfare centres on the size of the income support payments made to claimants. Less is heard of the other welfare state, which runs parallel to the 'traditional' welfare state, and is financed by tax concessions, such as mortgage interest relief and pension contribution relief. The Government has curtailed the growth in expenditure on the traditional welfare state, and, as has been seen, abolished some benefits and made real cuts in the value of others. However, no similar effort has been made to limit the growth of tax welfare. The overall effect has again been to widen still further the gap in living standards between those at either end of the income scale, and to expose still further the underclass, who benefit least from tax welfare. Indeed, there could be no greater contrast than that between the social security benefits that have been made liable to tax, and therefore reduced in value, and the way in which the Thatcher Governments have allowed the value of tax benefits to escalate. These benefits are not confined to mortgage interest relief and pension contribution relief; there are over a hundred. Here we look at the current cost of tax welfare.

Tax Benefits

The cost of the tax allowance welfare state has risen substantially. Mortgage interest relief, for example, which cost £1.25 billion a year in lost revenue at the time Mrs Thatcher was elected in 1979, is currently running at a total of £6.5 billion annually. One reason for this increased loss of revenue to the Exchequer has been the raising of the ceiling on the size of mortgages that qualify for tax subsidies. The

1983 budget increased the ceiling from £25,000 to £30,000, on the grounds that the lower limit was 'beginning to hinder a growing number of families who want to buy their first home, or to move' (*Hansard*, 15 March 1983, cols 145–6). Another, more important reason for the escalating cost of this form of welfare has been the increasing number of people buying their own home. A third factor in the huge growth in this welfare budget is the rapid rise in interest rates. A rise of 1 per cent in interest rates adds £400–500 million annually to the cost of mortgage tax relief. Paradoxically, the tax subsidy cushions the borrower from the full effects of a restrictive monetary policy. From June 1988 until February 1989 interest rates rose by 3.75 percentage points, but a quarter of this cost was borne not by the borrower but by the Exchquer. In order to restrict consumer credit by a given amount, the Government is forced to raise interest rates to a higher level than it would have to in a non-subsidized market. Conversely, the higher the rate of interest, the greater the additional cost to industry of financing new capital investment.

Mortgage interest relief is not the only tax subsidy available to houseowners. The revenue lost through exempting the sale of an individual's home from capital gains has risen from £1.5 billion to £2.6 billion since 1979. The third subsidy to owner occupation comes from the abolition of the Schedule A tax. Calculated on the imputed rent of the building, a rough updating of the tax suggests that, had it still been in effect today, something in the region of £1.3 billion would be raised annually. The public subsidy to home ownership from these two tax benefits, plus the abolition of Schedule A, is now over £10.5 billion per annum.

Tax benefits to private pension arrangements have risen at a similar rate, although the growth has been from a smaller base. The total subsidy to private pensions amounted to £9.8 billion in 1987–8. This sum equals more than half the entire health and personal social security budget. The main cost of this benefit comes from the subsidy to approved pension schemes costing £1.6 billion in 1987–8; subsidizing employers' contributions to funded pension schemes (£2.9 billion); exempting investment income of occupational pension schemes (£4.1 billion); and exempting lump sum payments (£1.2 billion).

A key fact about the tax benefit welfare state is that those on the highest incomes gain most. The distribution of mortgage interest tax relief, which stood at £4.9 billion before the rise in lending rates during the second half of 1988, is indicative of all tax benefits. Of the

2.4 million taxpayers earning less than £4,000 a year, or 11 per cent of all taxpayers, only 0.5 million are eligible for relief, and this group gain an average tax benefit of £110 a year, or 1 per cent of the entire benefit. At the top end of the income range, of the 430,000 taxpayers earning over £30,000 a year, 250,000 claim tax relief. This group represent 2 per cent of all taxpayers, yet gain an average payment of £1,480, or 8 per cent of the total cost of the benefit.

The extent to which a planned use of tax benefits reduces a recipient's tax burden is illustrated in the answer to a Parliamentary Question tabled by Gordon Brown, relating to the 1986–7 tax year. Married workers on a salary of £30,000 and £100,000 a year paid a marginal tax rate of 38.9 per cent and 51.2 per cent, respectively, on these earnings, if no tax allowances were claimed, other than personal ones. However, once the £100,000-a-year worker made an annual investment of £40,000 of his earnings under the Business Expansion Scheme, claimed mortgage tax relief on a £30,000 loan, made an annual investment of £5,000 into an approved pension scheme and a £1,000 life assurance premium, his marginal tax rate fell, from 51.2 per cent to 21.6 per cent. The £30,000-a-year worker, making a £5,000 investment under the Business Expansion Scheme, together with relief on a £30,000 mortgage, £1,500 into an approved pension scheme and a £200 annual premium for a life assurance policy, reduced his marginal tax rate from 38.9 per cent to 19 per cent. The man or woman on average earnings, with no tax benefits other than the personal tax allowance, faced a marginal tax rate of 28.5 per cent in 1986–7.

Summary

Half of all personal income is exempted from taxation as a result of the hundred or so tax allowances, or, more accurately, tax benefits. While the vast majority of those in work claim the relevant personal allowances – such as the single person's or the married man's tax allowance – even these are of most value to high earners who are able to set the allowances against the top rate of tax for which they are liable. The other tax benefits are even more clearly linked to income, with those on highest income claiming the lion's share of their value. Tax benefits are consumer led, unlike traditional welfare payments, which are subject to the Government's control of public expenditure.

Over the post decade, tax welfare has played an increasingly important part in boosting the living standards of the rich, while welfare cuts have reduced the income of those at the bottom of the pile.

CONCLUSION

Some people believe that Adam Smith's 'hidden hand' is at work in society, bringing about the most favourable productive outcome from the economy. A more appropriate image of Britain as it approaches the twenty-first century is of the economy governed by a not-so-hidden engine, working for greater inequality, both in rewards and life chances. The power of this engine can be seen during the decades following World War Two, when, despite a bipartisan political approach aimed at mitigation, class differences on many fronts remained as wide as ever. Since 1979, it has been the declared aim of the Government to 'let the children grow tall'. In operating an incomes policy on low pay, by changing the incidence of taxation on income and wealth, by cutting the rise in the welfare budget, while letting tax welfare be consumer led, the Government has brought about a revolutionary polarization in income and living standards, which can now be seen not only in the official data on income distribution, but also in widening class differences. Individually, none of these developments are responsible for the advent of an underclass. Taken together, with rise of mass unemployment, the explanation becomes more comprehensive. The developments described in this section will continue to have a cumulative impact, and, as differences in income, wealth and welfare are widened still further, Britain's underclass will become even more vulnerable, particularly when part of this strategy may disenfranchise this group from citizenship. Simultaneously, other forces have been at work, locking or fixing the underclass into place. Our discussion now turns to this aspect of contemporary Britain.

Part III

Fixing the Underclass

The emergence of an underclass in Britain is no accident. The significant increase in the number of people without work, the exclusion of the very poorest from the country's rapidly rising living standards, the hardening of attitudes towards this group amongst those who feel they are 'making it', together with the Thatcher Governments' determination to widen class differences, are the root causes. Nor will this underclass disappear without the implementation of a series of policies aimed at re-establishing full citizenship. The strategy will also require measures to counter the six forces currently at work locking this underclass firmly into place, and which are considered in this section.

The first is the dramatic increase in unemployment and the concentration of recent job losses on those at the bottom of the social hierarchy. Second, while the post-war upward social mobility for working-class youths has continued, this is now paralleled by a downward social mobility, out of the working class into unemployment. Third, the major restructuring taking place in the labour market is increasing the number of part-time, temporary and often low-paid jobs, while the numbers of full-time and better-paid jobs have declined. Fourth, the interaction of the tax and benefits system, which gives rise to the poverty and unemployment 'traps', operates to destroy the initiative of many poor people. Fifth, the Thatcher Governments have made major changes to owner-occupation and share ownership and this has resulted in many small wealth holders believing that their interests are now more closely allied with the rich, to the exclusion of people on low incomes. Moreover, the resulting decline in council housing has begun to lead to the rise of the ghetto. Sixth, the Thatcher Government's pension reforms will result in a return to a 'cradle to grave' condition of unremitted low income for the most disadvantaged.

11

Unemployment

Unemployment locks the underclass into place in three ways: it is more likely to hit those who are poor; the poorest are likely to be unemployed longest; and, in addition, instead of compensating the unemployed, the welfare state penalizes them more than any other group on welfare.

Hitting the Poor the Hardest

Unemployment does not fall gently and evenly across the whole population. It hits hardest those who are poorest, and, in this group, those who are struck by unemployment suffer the penalties for longer and longer periods. Nicholas Bosenquet was one of the first to demonstrate the unequal impact of unemployment. Analysing the 1966 data, at a time when the average level of unemployment stood at 2.6 per cent, he found that the rate for professional workers and those in supervisory grades was 0.6 and 1.3 per cent, respectively ('Is there a dual labour market in Great Britain?', *Economic Journal*, vol. 84, 1973). At the other end of the scale, the unemployment rate for personal services and unskilled manual workers was 4.9 and 6.8 per cent, respectively. This differential impact has worsened with the rapid rise in unemployment.

Adrian Sinfield has brought this analysis up to date by using data from the General Household Survey for 1975–7 and 1984 to measure the proportion of different social groups experiencing unemployment (Press notice, 30 March 1987). The unemployment rate for male professional workers, employers and managers has increased from 4 per cent in 1975–7 to 6 per cent in 1983–4. For semi-skilled and unskilled manual workers, the proportion of members experiencing unemployment almost doubled: from 18 to 32 per cent.

Using the same source of information, Sinfield looked at how unemployment has disproportionately affected blacks and young whites, the two groups from which many members of the underclass are being drawn. In 1975–7, 9 per cent of young white workers had been unemployed during a twelve-month period. By 1983–4 the proportion so affected had risen to 17 per cent. For black workers, the figures are 17 and 27 per cent, respectively. Moreover, workers aged between 18 and 24 in 1975–7 were more than twice as likely as older workers to experience unemployment, and this ratio has been maintained despite the massive increase in the numbers of unemployed during the following decade. In 1983–4, 33 per cent of young workers told interviewers from the GHS that they were unemployed or had experienced unemployment during the previous twelve months.

These findings from the GHS are averages for the whole country, and underestimate the seriousness of long-term unemployment for young people in those areas most affected by unemployment. In the North, for example, a team from Leicester University's Labour Market Studies Group has found that job prospects are so bleak that clear signs of an underclass are apparent for those for whom 'normal morality is inverted and educational achievement is undervalued'. Interviewing people aged between eighteen and twenty-four in Sunderland, the team found 31 per cent of males and 26 per cent of females had *never* had full-time paid employment. Figures for the equivalent groups studied in St Albans, in the South-East, were 3 per cent. The team found whole communities in Sunderland for whom unemployment was a way of life, and among whom a

new 'culture' was emerging. . . . People who have to exist on social security [over a long period of time] have a different set of values. Morality starts to change. Small scale thieving is seen as part of everyday life. (*Observer*, 25 January, 1987).

The Poor are Without Jobs the Longest

As the dole queues have lengthened, so too has the time the unemployed have been without work. The growth in the numbers who have been without work for a year or more has been perhaps the most disturbing aspect of today's unemployment, despite the Department of Employment's interviewing of all the long-term unemployed, and the Government's recent recognition of the need to direct job appointments at those who have been standing in the queue longest. In 1958, with unemployment at 408,000, the numbers of long-term unemployed stood at 38,700, or 9.5 per cent of the total. In 1968, when unemployment had passed the half-million mark, the long-term unemployed total stood at 88,400, or 16.5 per cent of the total. The most recent figures show a dramatic change, with the proportion of long-term unemployed now constituting a disturbing 41 per cent of all unemployed people. By April 1986, 186,711 men had been without work for more than five years, a sum nearly five times greater than the same group four decades earlier. Fewer women register for Unemployment Benefit, so their rate of unemployment is heavily disguised.

The poorest people experience the longest periods of being out of work. The longer a person (here defined as the head of the household) is unemployed, the more likely it is that he or she will belong to the general labourer or other occupational groups. Of managerial and professional workers unemployed in 1985, 18.1 per cent had been without work for up to six months, compared to 12.2 per cent of those who had been without a job for between two and three years. The equivalent figures for manual workers other than general labourers show a reverse pattern. While 39 per cent of those unemployed for up to six months were manual workers, this group made up almost half the unemployed who had been without work for between two and three years.

In fact, the Labour Force Survey underestimates the extent of this discrimination. Those who have been unemployed for three or more years are not asked about their previous employment, and are thereby excluded from the survey. Similarly, because the LFS considers the number of weeks a person has been without work since their previous job, those who have never had a job are also excluded. The evidence cited earlier shows that it is those from the poorest homes who are most likely to fall in either of these categories.

One reason why the poorest endure unemployment longest is that their share of the job market is shrinking, while those from higher social groups confront radically different job prospects. From 1979 to 1986, the number of people in full-time employment fell by 1.25 million (*Hansard*, 4 February 1987, cols 683–4). During the same period, the Department of Employment Labour Force Survey shows professionals, employers and managers as a group increasing their share of the total labour force: from 14.7 to 19.1 per cent. Meanwhile, the semi-skilled and unskilled manual workers' share of the much smaller total of numbers in full-time work fell by over 3 percentage points: from 26.7 to 23.3 per cent.

This finding is confirmed by the vacancy figures (that is, the number of job vacancies that are officially notified). Since the counting of unemployment was transferred from Job Centres to Unemployment Benefit Offices in November 1982, the Government has ceased carrying out an analysis of vacancies by occupation. However, recent estimates have been made by Adrian Sinfield and Neil Fraser on the assumption that the current occupational distribution of the unemployed, and of unfilled vacancies, has not changed since they were last published, in 1982 and 1985, respectively (note supplied by Adrian Sinfield and Neil Fraser, 1 June 1987). The evidence already cited on the worsening position of the poorest in the unemployment stakes suggests that these assumptions will lead to an underestimate of the difficulties the poor have in finding work. Even so, by 1987, the Sinfield and Fraser estimate shows an overall ratio of eighteen unemployed to every job vacancy. For the general labourer category, the figure stands at 177. Once a person has become unemployed for any length of time, the chances are that he or she will continue to be unemployed. The reason for this is quite simple. As the researchers from Leicester University noted, the unemployed

become cut off from the world of work. . . . They don't hear about job opportunities because these are mostly passed around by word of mouth among those who are in work. So the unemployed, living on social security, usually on big council estates, are cut off from the rest of society. (*Observer*, 25 January 1987)

The Unemployed are Penalized Most

It is this hard core of unemployed – that is, those who have been out of work longest – that makes up a large part of the new underclass. It is not only the length of time that someone has been unemployed that is important, but also the fact that it affects a person's lifetime income. Both young and old, people are punished in a number of ways for the failure to achieve. First, because the dole is significantly below earning levels, the income of the unemployed drops, often dramatically. As mentioned above, income support only has an ordinary, and not a long-term rate. Instead of this two tier rate, claimants may qualify for premiums – if they are disabled or have children, for example. While this move is more favourable than supplementary benefit was to some of the unemployed, the new system discriminates heavily against the young, single unemployed. Second, other parts of the social security system actively discriminate against the unemployed. Unemployment benefit is limited to only one year, and, unlike other national insurance benefits, such as an old-age pension, cannot be drawn for as long as needed. Moreover, unemployment benefit is paid at a lower rate, and, for a married couple, is valued at only 54 per cent of the level of the pension paid to a retired couple. The earnings-related supplement, which was introduced in 1966 so that the value of unemployment benefit would more accurately reflect the income that a claimant enjoyed while employed, has been abolished. Finally, a lack of work often excludes claimants from occupational pension schemes, which, together with owner-occupation, constitute one of the two most important forms of capital accumulation for the majority of the population.

Summary

The current high level of unemployment has been crucial in bringing an underclass into existence. As the number of jobs in manufacturing has fallen, people who could previously expect full-time work have found themselves excluded from paid employment, often for considerable periods. Moreover, unemployment has not been evenly distributed. It has fallen most heavily and for the longest periods on the most vulnerable members of society, with a particular concentration on the young, and on unskilled or semi-skilled workers. It should come as little surprise that some of those who feel they have no stake in 'official' society should react in a way that demonstrates their exclusion. It is important not to lose sight of the fact that the main aim of this non-revolutionary group is to win a place back in society by gaining a job.

The disenfranchising effect of unemployment has worked on a number of fronts. In financial terms, the income of the unemployed drops, usually by a significant amount. This is likely to cripple a person's ability to follow his or her group's round of normal social activities. Moreover, not having a job strikes at that aspect of citizenship which involves the carrying out of social duties, one of which is to earn a living for oneself and one's family. Unemployment also disenfranchises in other ways. Those without work are excluded from building up savings, whether in the form of a house or an adequate pension, and thereby gaining a stake in society. Unemployment has also had an important effect on the direction of social mobility.

12

Two-way Social Mobility

One of the dominant social characteristics of Britain over the past fifty years has been the degree of upward social mobility of those whose parents held traditional working-class jobs. This upward movement in the social hierarchy by many working-class boys (significantly, none of the studies has looked at girls) has not been achieved at the expense of the opportunities of children from middle-class backgrounds, but by an explosion in the number of middle-class jobs – or an expansion in the service class or the salariat. This predominantly one-directional social mobility was the pattern up until the quadrupling of oil prices in the winter of 1973–4, an event which, for the purposes of this book, is accepted as marking the end of the post-war period in Britain. Since that time, a major change has occurred with respect to social mobility that has had a direct bearing on the emergence of Britain's underclass, and this is considered in this chapter. The Nuffield study on the direction of social mobility from the 1930s is considered, together with the latest updating of this work following the 1983 election. The recent sharp rise in the number of unemployed people is also taken into account. The effect of the growth in school leaving qualifications on the success of the least qualified in the job market is examined, together with the role of the various Government training schemes for the young unemployed school-leaver. To understand the significance of these most recent changes, it is first necessary to review the main trends in social mobility in Britain over the past fifty years, before considering those developments that have become more marked since the mid-1970s.

Pattern of Mobility

There have been a number of major studies measuring the degree of social mobility in British society, the most recent of which was carried out in 1972 by Nuffield College, Oxford. This survey, which examined the degree of social mobility in Britain from the period prior to World War Two, came to three major conclusions.

The first was that, from the inter-war years up to the year of the study, men of *all* class origins have become progressively more likely to move into professional, administrative and managerial positions – or into the service class of modern British society. Matching this change, the survey shows that men from working-class backgrounds were less likely than their fathers to be found holding manual wage-earning positions. Second, the direction of social mobility was largely, though not exclusively, an upward one, due to the change in the structure of the class system itself; the service class continued to grow while the manual working class contracted. Third, downward mobility from positions in the service class to other class positions has steadily decreased over the same time span (A. H. Halsey, A. F. Heath and John Ridge, *Origins and Destinations*, Oxford University Press, 1980).

Material collected for the study on the 1983 general election has been used by two researchers, John Goldthorpe and Clive Payne, to update the Nuffield study, and to examine the extent of social mobility a decade after the end of the post-war period (John H. Goldthorpe and Clive Payne, 'Trends in intergeneration class mobility in England and Wales, 1972–83', *Sociology*, vol. 20, no. 1, February 1986). The most significant change recorded between the 1972 and 1983 surveys has been the advent of mass unemployment. In 1972 the official unemployment rate was under 4 per cent, and of those questioned in the Nuffield survey, only 5 per cent told interviewers that they were currently out of work. This total included men who, although unemployed, were between jobs. By 1983, unemployment had reached over 12 per cent, and long-term unemployment (defined as being without work for over a year) had emerged as a significant economic and social issue. Almost 9 per cent of the men aged between twenty and sixty-four resident in England and Wales during the 1983 survey reported that they were unemployed, and this total excluded those who were waiting to take up jobs. Of the total sample, 5 per cent had been without work for more than a year.

Those unemployed in the 1972 survey had been classified by their last job. Goldthorpe and Payne believed it

would be unwise for us in analysing our 1983 data to treat the unemployed in the same way as in 1972 without at least considering whether this might not seriously distort our results; more specifically, it would seem important to examine what effect it would have on the 1983 mobility [results] if unemployment, or at all events long-term unemployment, were itself regarded as a mobility 'status' or outcome.   (p. 15)

The result of this special analysis

is something that might not have been anticipated: the principle finding concerning trends in class mobility since 1972 can stand unchanged even when in . . . 1983 . . . unemployment is regarded as a separate mobility status. That is to say, it still remains the case that men of all social origins have become more likely to be found in service-class positions and less likely to be found in working-class ones.   (p. 15)

It would be wrong to deduce from this conclusion that unemployment has had no effect on mobility. Unemployment is still largely a working-class experience. Not surprisingly, therefore, the results of the 1983 survey show that mass unemployment 'has created a serious new risk of what can only be regarded as downard social mobility – *and that risk is much greater for men in working class positions, by whatever route they come into them, than it is for others'* (p. 17). In 1972, less than 16 per cent of this age group had been found to be upwardly mobile as against 60 per cent who retained their working class positions (p. 18). Taking men of working-class origin of the same age group in 1983, and signifying unemployment as a separate category, the survey found 22 per cent were upwardly mobile, 40 per cent remained in working-class positions, while a further 11 per cent had been pushed down into unemployment, and over half of this last group had been without work for over a year. A decade after the end of the first post-war period in Britain (that is, during the sharp oil price rise mentioned above) social mobility was characterized both by heightening opportunities of rising socially, as well as increased risks of being caught in a downward spiral – particularly for those of working-class origin, who are among those who most easily fall prey to recruitment into the underclass.

Effect of Education Changes

This downard mobility is now being reinforced by educational changes that operate not only to prevent the most disadvantaged children from benefiting from the increased degree of upward social mobility, but also prevent many of them entering the labour market at all. Until recently, the crucial question centred on the role schools played in determining which children rise socially (Anthony Heath and John Ridge, 'Schools, examinations and occupational attainment', reprinted in *Achievement and Inequality in Education*, ed. Jane Purves and Margaret Hales, Routledge and Kegan Paul, London, 1983). Since the 1972 Nuffield Survey was carried out, three major educational changes have occurred. Comprehensive reorganization began in 1965, although most schools were not reorganized on this basis until the mid-1970s. The school-leaving age was raised to sixteen in 1974, thereby lessening the chance of pupils leaving school without the opportunity of taking qualifying examinations. Also, the advent of the CSE, and more recently the GCSE, has significantly changed the character of the output of secondary education. These changes mean that, in studying the emergence of Britain's underclass, it is necessary to change the focus of attention, away from the traditional topic of selection for secondary education, to one of selection at entry into the labour market.

The earlier mobility studies showed that access to the grammar school was crucial in gaining a service-type job. In the post-war period the acquisition of O-level certificates became similarly crucial in gaining a foothold onto a career in the growing service sector. A comparison between the 1972 and 1983 studies shows a large increase in the numbers from all social classes gaining O-level qualifications. But important changes are occurring now that 91 per cent of the children of working-class backgrounds gain similar qualifications. 'The likelihood here is that, as fast as the working class catches up at O level, qualifications required in the labour market will move upwards with A levels becoming the key qualifications for a successful career in the salariat' (Anthony Heath, 'Class in the classroom,' *New Society*, 17 July 1987, p. 15).

Children from working-class homes have now come under two new pressures. Those who compete successfully under what they saw as the rules of the game – that is, to obtain O-level qualifications, find the rules have changed; A levels had become the required entry into those jobs offering the greatest upward social mobility. But at the same time another pressure is being applied to the least gifted children from working-class homes. This new pressure, in fact, comes from the very success of more children gaining paper qualifications. This change puts at greater risk those working-class boys and girls who fail to acquire any such paper qualifications.

The subsequent growth and proportion obtaining O level, and even more so of those obtaining CSE, means that school-leavers are now more heterogeneous in their qualifications. The youngest group has in effect become more stratified in educational terms and there are now new gradations of educational attainment that mirror differences in social background. Whereas most working-class children were once alike in leaving school without qualification, differences are now emerging between the skilled and semi-skilled section of the working-class.   (p. 15)

As it is from the children of the semi- and unskilled working class who leave school without any qualification that the underclass is being recruited, it is important to ask which children are most likely to fall into this category. Chapter 3 detailed the educational performances of the poorest children. While some performed well – although not as well as their intellectual peers who were from better-off homes – the vast majority of the poorest children gained few, if any, qualifications from their schooling.

Training Schemes

Matching the change in the range of qualifications of school-leavers has been a dramatic transformation in the youth labour market in a little over a decade. Whereas in 1974 well over 60 per cent of male sixteen year olds were in work, today that total is only 16 per cent. For seventeen year olds the equivalent figures are 70 and 44 per cent. The changed outlook for young women workers is similar (see table 1 in 'Education and the labour market status of young people', *Employment Gazette*, September 1987, p. 460). Not surprisingly, therefore, with youth unemployment so high, some school-leavers with qualifications fail to find jobs. They, along with their peers who have no paper qualifications at all, compete for places on the Youth Training Schemes (YTS). These schemes, which originally ran for one year, have now been extended to two years. As 30 per cent of YTS graduates fail to find employment at the end of their course it is crucial to understand which groups are able to use the YTS to gain a foothold in the labour market, and those which are unsuccessful.

Those young people who gained places on what were called 'employer-led courses', or mode A courses, were the ones most likely to gain employment at the end of their training. Those young people undertaking YTS at colleges, or on community-based schemes, which were called mode B schemes, were less likely to be successful in entering the labour market when they graduated from their courses (see the transcript of the BBC TV *Panorama* programme 'Fair play for Britain's Blacks', 6 July 1987, p. 3). The differences between types of YTS schemes has now been eliminated on paper – but the differences in courses, whether employer led or not, and the outcome for employment, remain.

The Government does not publish any breakdown of the social background of those YTS graduates who fail to gain employment. Studies of how black youths fare after completing YTS have, however, been made public. While the underclass is composed of both black and white workers, black workers, in Elizabeth Burney's phrase, act as a barium meal in an X-ray – highlighting the weak points – or, for our purposes, the fate of the most disadvantaged, those most likely to find themselves in the ranks of the underclass.

Two such reports on the fate of black workers on the YTS have been published. A team of researchers from Bristol University was commissioned to examine what the YTS had to offer young black people and to indicate how they got on during the first six months of the scehme (S. Fenton, *Ethnic Minorities and the Youth Training Scheme* Research and Development Series, no. 20, MSC, 1984). This report was published along with a study by the Commission for Racial Equality (CRE) entitled *Racial Equality in the Youth Training Scheme* (CRE, 1984).

The most significant finding of these reports was of the over-representation of black youths on mode B schemes – or on schemes that were less likely than mode A schemes to lead to a job. (For a summary of the findings, see Steve Fenton and Paul Burton, 'YTS and equal opportunity policy', in *Black Youth Futures*, ed. Malcolm Cross and Douglas I. Smith, National Youth Bureau, 1987.) In some instances the researchers accepted that this pattern might be explained by the preponderance of mode B schemes 'but more often a process of "guided drift" could be detected, based on a stereotyping of both young people and mode delivery' (pp. 38–9).

Partly in response to these criticisms, the Youth Training Board (YTB) carried out a review of the training schemes during the summer of 1984. One aspect of this review was to examine whether the MSC's commitment to an equal opportunities policy was being fulfilled in both the letter and spirit of the agreement. The results of this review came to the disturbingly complacent conclusion that, as blacks experience discrimination generally in society, 'it would perhaps be more surprising if there was no evidence of discrimination' in YTS schemes (pp. 40–1).

Summary

Since the inter-war years, Britain has been for many people an upwardly mobile society, with children from working-class homes winning jobs in the expanding service class. Even with the advent of mass unemployment, this trend has continued, if anything more strongly. Unemployment, however, has brought about a simultaneous and contrary downward social movement. Those most likely to be caught in this new, downward flow are young people from the poorest homes. The means by which people are caught and recruited into the underclass has changed. Just as selection via the 11-plus, was the decisive influence, the gaining of school-leaving qualifications is now crucial in deciding who gains the best jobs. The most vulnerable young people now leave school without qualifications and are selected for the underclass through one of the Government's YTS schemes. While class-based information does not exist for all those students who fail to gain work after graduating from a YTS, the conclusion about how the scheme operates in the case of black youths is probably equally valid with respect to white youths without qualifications coming from poor, unskilled, working-class homes. Because the poorest are directed to those schemes least likely to result in gaining a job, they are in fact being selected for unemployment and possibly membership of the underclass at the end of their courses. This outcome of the YTS courses completes the process of marginalization to the fringes of society; from the poorest homes, to the poorest school performances, to the greatest difficulty obtaining work, to placement on those training schemes least likely to lead to full-time paid employment. Once in the adult world of work, the underclass faces further discrimination when it comes to selection for the primary or secondary labour market.

13

The Rise of Secondary Employment

The third force forging Britain's underclass stems from the labour market itself. The advent of mass unemployment has largely been brought about by the destruction of full-time jobs in manufacturing industry: a fall of 2 million since 1979 (*Hansard*, 30 November 1987, col. 398). As the number of full-time jobs has declined, there has also been an increase in the number of what are called 'flexible workers', that is temporary, part-time or home workers. The *Financial Times* reports that, by 1985, one in three of those in employment were in this category (*Financial Times*, 27 February 1987) and according to national estimates published by the Department of Employment early in 1987, the number of flexible workers rose by 16 per cent between 1981 and 1985, while those in permanent, full-time employment fell by 6 per cent.

This trend is likely to continue, restructuring the job market into two distinct tiers. It is important, of course, to recognize that the secondary, or flexible part of the labour market is itself neatly divided into two parts. One arises from the adaptation to new skills required to man the information technology revolution through which we are now living. The other is dominated by workers with few skills, other than their willingness to work the hours required by their employers. This discussion focuses on this second group. What chances there are of the underclass obtaining any work are largely confined to this secondary and flexible labour market, and that part which is characterized by less security of employment, low pay and little or no pension or fringe benefits. This section of the labour market is also virtually non-unionized, providing for almost no representation on pay and working conditions, or health and safety regulations.

The increase in the number of working women is disproportionately concentrated in this sector, and while the rates of pay are low, it would appear that many of these workers are, in fact, the main breadwinners. This chapter looks at the rise in the secondary labour market, studies what the future trends are likely to be, and examines how limited the scope of traditional trade union action will be in countering the consequences of this job market restructuring.

The Secondary Labour Market

An important part of this secondary labour market is composed of what are known as flexible workers. It is important to stress, however, that not all flexible workers can be classified in the same way. As well as the growth in the number of low-paid jobs, a significant group of flexible workers find themselves in great demand, and consequently gain high salaries. The secondary labour market considered here is made up of poorer-paid workers, undertaking part-time or home work. It also covers a number of those workers who appear in the self-employed statistics. The Government attaches a great deal of importance to this unprecedented growth in self-employment and small businesses: it is seen as the main drive to create an enterprise culture that will hopefully lead to an increase in the numbers in work. Yet the Government's own figures show that in most cases what has occurred is the creation of single-person businesses, that is self-employment by individual workers who do not employ any assistants as part of their business activities. It is for this reason that this group should be included in any study of the flexible workforce. Between 1981 and 1984, the number of those for whom self-employment was the main employment rose by almost 0.5 million to a little over 2.5 million – a growth to 11.2 per cent of the total employment figures.

The growth in part-time jobs from 1981 to 1985 records the smallest growth in the ranks of the flexible workforce – totalling no more than 300,000 for the whole period. This increase, however, needs to be seen in a longer time-scale. In the two decades up to 1981, the numbers in part-time work *doubled* to over 4 million, while the numbers in full-time employment fell by 2 million. By the spring of 1985, 4.5 million, or 21.7 per cent of all those in employment, were in part-time jobs, and the UK currently employs over 40 per cent of all part-time workers in the EEC (Income Data Services *Part-timers, Temps and Job Sharers*, April 1985).

The third part of the flexible workforce is composed of those undertaking what is called 'temporary work'. While a range of jobs now make up this sector, they neatly divide into seasonal, temporary or casual work on the one hand, and, on the other, work contracted for a fixed period of time or for whatever time it takes to complete a defined task. Agency and professional workers are to be found in this second category. When temporary workers responding to the British Labour Force Survey were themselves invited to differentiate between these two groups, two-thirds placed themselves in the first category. Members of this, the larger group of temporary workers, were most likely to be unskilled or semi-skilled.

A special analysis of the overall extent of the temporary workforce carried out on the British/European Communities' Labour Force Survey bears on the changing structure of the labour market and its likely repercussions on the outlook for Britain's underclass. While a higher proportion of temporary workers than of the total labour force were found to be women workers (6 per cent compared to 41 per cent), temporary workers were also 'considerably younger' than the generality of workers, largely because a high proportion of the former are still teenagers. One in five were found to be under twenty and 'a quarter of all teenagers in the labour force work on a temporary basis' (B. Casey, 'The extent and nature of temporary employment in Great Britain', *Policy Studies*, vol. VIII, part 1, July 1987, p. 67). Many, although not all of these young workers would be occupying relatively low-skilled positions. Of concern for future employment prospects was the finding that the 'extent of formal training given by employing organisations was usually minimal' (p. 73). While there has been a dispute about how quickly, if at all, this temporary sector of employment is on the increase, the results of the Spring 1985 Labour Force Survey are unequivocal about the extent and direction of change. They reveal an enormous growth in this sector. The number of temporary workers rose from 621,000 in 1981 (including some people on Government schemes) to 1,314,000 in 1985 (excluding people on Government schemes).

Commenting on the Labour Force Survey results, Catherine Hakim remarks: 'The importance of the "flexible" sector has clearly been underestimated; it is hardly a narrow and insignificant fringe on the edges of the labour market' ('Homeworking in Britain: key findings from the national survey of home-based workers', *Employment Gazette*, February 1987, from which all of the above relevant information has been taken). Hakim concludes by observing that: 'By the mid-1980's, the labour force divided neatly into two-thirds "permanet" and one-third "flexible". On this measure, one quarter of all men in work, and half of all women in work are now in the sector offering numerical flexibility' (p. 93).

Future Trends

This marked trend, from 'inflexible' to 'flexible', and from manufacturing to the service sector, will continue, according to a study published in 1986 by the Institute of Manpower Studies. In that year, the IMS estimated a further 650,000 job losses in manufacturing between 1985 and 1990 being only partly counterbalanced by the creation of 500,000 jobs in the private service sector. In a further study published a year later, the IMS considered in detail seven private sector service industries identified as the fastest growing job creators: retailing, wholesaling, hotels and catering, banking, building societies, insurance and business services. Commenting on the report, the *Financial Times* remarked that these sectors are identified as dominating the thrust towards a post-industrial society, and as:'spearheading the second industrial revolution, and settling employment trends, such as part-time working, job sharing and decentralisation' (*Financial Times*, 5 February, 1987). Three sectors in particular are identified as the predominant job creators to the end of the decade: business services (215,000 jobs), hotel and catering (120,000 jobs) and wholesale distribution (70,000 jobs).

This trend towards a greater reliance upon jobs in service industries does not by itself, however, hold out a great deal of hope for the long-term male unemployed, or the emerging underclass. The main beneficiaries of the new jobs in this sector are likely to be female: it is forecast that they will gain two-thirds of these jobs. Part-time workers will claim about a third of the projected increases, while young workers gain only about one quarter of the jobs. On the other hand, the number of part-time female employees alone is likely to increase by an estimated 122,000 during this period. About 10 per cent of the new jobs are likely to go to the self-employed, most of them coming from the ranks of those already in employment. Moreover, a significant proportion of the jobs are likely to be low paid. Hotels and catering are notorious for their low rates of pay. Low pay is also common in wholesale distribution and, when the details of the job become available, this many also apply to business services.

In its conclusions to the study, the IMS sounds another note of caution. While the seven sectors examined were expected to continue to create jobs until the end of the decade, that rate of increase is predicted to be lower than in the recent past, as new technology and industrial concentration increase productivity. Significantly, the study draws attention to one of the causes of fairly rapid growth in these sectors, namely the transfer of jobs from the production industries as contracting out to the service industries continues.

To say that we are in the midst of a second industrial revolution, propelled by a rapid growth in services is not a misnomer; this growth has been exceptional since 1975. However, the claim begins to look exaggerated in the context of the causes of the growth; in particular, the contracting out of services from the productive industries.

The IMS's final comment is important: 'If economic revolutions are about wealth creation rather than redistribution, this latest one still has a long way to go' (*'Services: the second industrial revolution?'* by Amin Rajan, Report by the Institute of Manpower Services Group, Butterworths, reported in the *Financial Times*, 5 February 1987).

The trend towards privatization, or contracting out, not only results in jobs being reclassified from one industrial sector to another, but often to a substantial growth in the numbers of part-time, low-paid positions. I quote the case of my own area of the Wirral, again not because it is unique, but rather for the very opposite reason. Here, as elsewhere, hospital cleaning services were won by a private contractor. Workers who had previously had full-time jobs, security of employment and a full range of fringe benefits, including the right to an occupational pension, were offered part-time employment at a lower hourly rate of pay without any occupational pension entitlement. For most of the workers previously employed by the health authority, their social security entitlement became higher than the wages they could gain from such part-time employment.

Trade Union Weakness

A further change in the nature of the labour market is being brought about by the decline in the strength of the trade unions. In part, this decline has been effected by the successful ideological battle waged against them by Mrs Thatcher. For the time being at least, she has managed to change the attitude of a significant proportion of the population towards the legitimacy of crucial parts of normal trade union practice, although opinion polls now show a growing esteem for trade unions shorn of some of the pre-1979 powers.

Trade union strength has also been curtailed by the rise in unemployment and the consequent fall in the number of trade unionists. This decline has been faster than the decline in employment, dropping from 13.3 million in 1979, to 10.7 million in 1985, a 19.5 per cent decline since 1979. The fall in employment has been much more marked amongst male than female workers and this has affected the composition of union membership; females now comprise almost 35 per cent of the entire membership. Generally speaking, female workers are less likely to undertake traditional forms of industrial action, and this may have a growing impact on the role of the labour movement in future decades.

Here a note of caution should perhaps be added about the conventional wisdom that falling membership automatically leads to a decrease in trade union influence. 'Depending on what set of figures you employ, it is possible to arrive at quite different estimates of the impact of the recession on trade unions', writes Dr John Kelly, a labour economist (reported in the *Financial Times*, 11 November 1987). The figures often used in public debate measure trade union density against the number of employees in employment plus the unemployed. Such data are relevant when looking at the impact trade unions may be able to have on the national political process. But in the local bargaining situation, trade union strength is more effectively measured in terms of their following in the workplace.

Despite these cautionary remarks, it appears unlikely that union power will revive as soon as the economic climate improves. In a new study on the future of trade unions, P. F. Beaumont examines a number of structural forces, all of which are working against a re-establishment of the growing status quo ante (see *The Decline of Trade Union Organisations*, Croom Helm, Beckenham, 1987). The main forces that work against trade union interest, according to Beaumont, are the difficulties experienced by unions in using the favourable industrial relations procedures laid down by the last Labour Government; moves in the public sector that have made trade union organization difficult, and, in the case of GCHQ, unlawful; and the

Conservative Government's continuing drive against the closed shop.

The study also draws on existing published data about current practices and predictions about where growth in jobs is most likely to take place, as a basis for projections on likely trade union growth. Such an analysis reveals, firstly, that the industrial relations 'pace-setters' in the UK are no longer the large corporations that establish paternalistic relations with trade unions, but are, instead, predominantly non-trade union companies, of which Marks and Spencer is a prime example. Second, past trends in Scotland and North-West England suggest that a relatively high proportion of newly established firms are non-union, and this is particularly so in new-town locations. By and large, these new firms are: 'overwhelmingly British-owned, single, independent establishments of relatively small size', in which employee relations are generally seen as involving good informal communications and flexible working practices (quoted in the *Financial Times*, 20 February 1987).

Similar findings on the decline in the strength of trade unions has been highlighted in a report on labour performance in the North-West – an area traditionally strong in trade union organization. Surveying 150 companies – half UK owned and half foreign owned – it was found that while 69 per cent of companies recognized trade unions for the purpose of collective bargaining, non-recognition was higher in the newer industries, i.e., those likely to supply most of the new employment in the decades ahead.

Summary

Whatever the causes, the rise in part-time work has had a profound effect on the employment conditions and prospects of a growing number of workers. While for some this is a welcome development, for many others this structural change in the labour market reduces the income and the company welfare benefits of those concerned to such an extent that they are made inferior to their colleagues in the primary labour market. All too often, flexible working also entails the loss of entitlement to an adequate occupational pension, and hence the possibility of real hardship during retirement. The lack of security of employment makes flexible working a kind of half-way house, and this half-way house contains a number of workers struggling to keep themselves from dropping into the abyss of the underclass. Being *in* work, no matter how poor the conditions, opens up the possibility of recruitment into the primary labour market. Being part of the secondary market, however, carries a substantial risk of being pushed back into unemployment, and possibly into the ranks of the underclass. The likelihood of the trade unions being able to counter these trends is non-existent, despite the brave attempts by some trade union leaders to convince potential recruits otherwise. In addition, the secondary labour market also poses major incentive problems, and these are now considered.

14

Destroying Initiative

The fourth way in which the underclass is immobilized at the bottom of our society has been through the spread of means-tested assistance, which has a devastating effect on the initiative of people on low incomes. A combination of means-tested assistance being withdrawn as income rises, together with an increased tax bill, has created a particular disincentive for those of the poor who try and improve their own position by personal effort and initiative. This disincentive usually goes under the name of the 'poverty trap'. Similarly, for those workers moving off unemployment pay and into work, the effects of tax, loss of income support, plus the additional cost of going to work, have given rise to what is called the 'unemployment trap'. Each of these traps is considered in this chapter, which begins by examining the increase in the numbers subjected to means-tested assistance in recent years.

Means Tests

In 1948, the old Poor Law was abolished. In its place, the Attlee Government instituted a range of national insurance benefits – such as old-age pension, unemployment pay and sickness benefit – together with a scheme of national assistance. The aim was that as a greater number of the population became eligible for national insurance benefits, fewer people would be dependent on the safety net of national assistance to provide them with a minimum income. As we saw in Part I, the opposite has occurred. Throughout the post-war period, there has been an increase in the numbers dependent on means-tested national assistance, or, as it was called from 1966, supplementary benefit. In 1948, a little less than a million households were drawing national assistance. By 1979, the number had risen to 2.8 million. The increase in the numbers claiming benefit since 1979, is, as was pointed out in Part I, greater than the whole of the increase in the years up to the election of the first Thatcher Government. By November 1979, there were 2.8 million regular payments of supplementary benefit, and these payments determined the living standards of 4.4 million people. The equivalent figures for May 1987 are 4.9 million claimants, and 8.2 million people dependent on supplementary benefit (*Hansard*, 25 November 1987, col. 245).

Throughout the 1960s, local authorities introduced rebate schemes for council tenants unable to meet their full rent. Accompanying this measure was a national scheme, operated by the local authorities, for rate-payers unable to meet a full rates bill. During 1981–2, the year before the national housing benefit scheme came into operation, 1.6 million tenants gained rent rebates, a further 250,000 tenants in private property gained a rent allowance, and 3.7 million rate-payers gained rate rebates. When these local authority schemes were standardized into the national housing benefit scheme, the numbers claiming a rent rebate or a rate rebate increased to 3.26 and 5.3 million, respectively (*Hansard*, 13 July 1987, col. 373).

Simultaneously with the preparation of the new housing benefit scheme, the Government began operating a policy of significantly increasing the level of council house rents, and a threefold increase has occurred in the nine years since 1979 (House of Commons Library Note, 19 July 1988). Not surprisingly, therefore, the numbers of people eligible for housing benefit increased, and so did the total cost of the scheme. By 1985–6, the numbers claiming rent rebates had increased to 4 million, the numbers claiming rent allowances to 1.2 million, and the number of householders claiming rate rebates to 7.3 million. While continuing a policy of pushing up rents, the Government began to curtail expenditure on the housing benefit scheme, and by 1987–8 the numbers claiming rent rebates had fallen to 3.7 million, and those claiming rate rebates to 7.1 million. The numbers claiming rent allowances had marginally increased to 1.2 million (*Hansard*, 13 July 1987, col. 373). By April 1990 the Government intends to replace the system of local rates with a community charge. The poll tax will increase the numbers eligible for housing benefit. In the Green Paper, *Paying for Local Government* (Cmnd. 9714), the Government estimated that the housing benefit case-load in Britain would rise by over 1 million when the community charge is fully in place (*Hansard*, 10 November 1987, col. 153).

The Conservative Party went into the 1970 election with a pledge to increase family allowances (renamed child benefit in 1979). In the event, the Heath Government introduced a new means-tested benefit, called Family Income Supplement (FIS), which could be claimed by working families on low incomes. By 1979, there were 77,000 recipients of FIS, and these payments helped determine the family income of 214,000 people. The equivalent figures by April 1986 were 200,000 and 530,000, respectively (*Hansard*, 9 February 1988, col. 186w). In 1988, FIS was replaced by family credit. This benefit is more generous than FIS, many more people are eligible to claim, and the average value of payments is expected to be significantly higher than under FIS.

Table 14.1 brings together the available information on the growth in the numbers of people dependent on means-tested welfare. Unfortunately, it is not possible to state what the overall dependency total is, as most supplementary benefit claimants will also be drawing housing benefit. Even so, the direction of change is clear – a massive increase

Table 14.1 *Numbers claiming means-tested assistance, 1979 and 1986 (thousands)*

	1979		1986	
	Claimants	*Claimants and dependents*	*Claimants*	*Claimants and dependants*
Supplementary Benefit	2,855	4,860	4,370	8,164
Family Income Support	77	214	200	530
Housing Benefit				
Rent	1,425	NA	4,910	NA
Rates[a]	3,065	NA	7,135	NA

NA, not available.

[a] Most recipients of rent rebates/allowances also receive rate rebates. Rate rebate recipients include owner-occupiers.

Source *Hansard*, 25 November 1987, col. 245 and *Hansard*, 13 July 1988, col. 373.

in seven years of the numbers caught in the means-test trap. The number claiming help with their rent jumped from 1.4 million to 5 million, and the number gaining help with their rates has grown from 3 million to over 7 million (again, there is an overlap between these two groups). There are no details on the number of dependents, as opposed to claimants of housing benefit. Data on dependants is available for supplementary benefit, and, as noted above, the number has shot up from 4.4 million to 8.2 million.

Just how important a role means-tested assistance plays in the Government's overall strategy is seen not only in the numbers claiming this form of social security, but in its growing share of public expenditure. Expenditure on national insurance benefits, benefits for which claimants become entitled because of their contribution record, covering a range of help from unemployment to old-age pensions, has risen by 400 per cent over the past thirty-five years up to 1984–5. Expenditure on what are termed non-contributory benefits, benefits paid to whole groups of claimants irrespective of their level of income, such as invalidity benefit and the attendance allowance, has risen by 290 per cent. While the increase in both these benefits is substantial, it is dwarfed by the increase in money spent on means-tested benefits such as supplementary benefit and housing benefit. These benefits have recorded a 1,010 per cent increase since 1949–50. This increase has, however, largely occurred since 1979. Not surprisingly, therefore, whereas in 1949–50 means-tested benefits accounted for only 12.7 per cent of the social security budget, they now command over a quarter of all social security expenditure (*Reform of Social Security: Background Papers*, Cmnd. 9519, pp. 28–9). It is against this background – of the growing importance that the Government attaches to means-tested assistance – seen both in its rising share of public expenditure, and the significant rise in the numbers claiming such assistance, that we need to consider the operation of the poverty and unemployment traps.

Poverty Trap

The poverty trap has been brought about by the interaction of the paying of tax and the loss of means-tested assistance on each £1 of additional earnings. Particularly important in this respect is family credit, which replaces FIS. In its extreme form, the poverty trap resulted in a situation where a £1 increase in income from work resulted in a reduction in net income, that is the worker was faced with a marginal tax rate in excess of 100 per cent (for the first use of the term, see Frank Field and David Piachaud, *New Statesman*, 3 December 1971).

There is no single point in the income scale where the poverty trap begins to operate. Because family credit and housing benefit are withdrawn over a large band of income, and because low-income families begin to pay tax at a low threshold, there are now whole bands of income over which it is difficult for low-income families to improve their net income. For example, a family with four dependent children on gross earnings of £75 per week, paying average rent and local authority rates, would gain an income of £123.25 per week, after taking into account means-tested assistance. However, to raise this income to £140.90 per week the family would need to more than double their earnings, from £75 a week to £165 a week (*Hansard*, 28 July 1988, col. 509).

Over the past decade or so, there has been evidence to show that an increasing number of low-paid families in work were caught in the poverty trap. In 1974, the loss of FIS and the payment of tax and national insurance amounted to an 89 per cent marginal tax rate. In that year, according to a report from the Treasury and Civil Service Select Committee, of the 75,210 FIS recipients, only 15,000, or 20 per cent, were estimated to be above the tax threshold when FIS was claimed in the previous year (Treasury and Civil Service Committee, *The Structure of Personal Income, Taxation and Income Support*, House of Commons Paper 2021, HMSO 1982, table 11, p. 15). By 1986, however, there was a total of 200,000 families in receipt of FIS, and of these, 69 per cent were paying both tax and national insurance contributions, and 25 per cent were paying national insurance contributions only (*Hansard*, 23 February, 1987, col. 128). The Government estimates that 78 per cent of families drawing family credit are currently above the tax threshold (*Hansard*, 29 July 1988, cols 823–4w). So, not only are more families drawing family credit than FIS, but a larger proportion of this group pays tax and insurance on each additional £1 of earnings, as well as losing part of the family credit payment.

One of the aims of the Government's 1988 benefit reforms was to ensure that no working families were faced with a marginal tax rate of over 100 per cent. This objective has been met, but at a price; an increasing number of poor families are faced with high marginal tax rates. At the current time, the vast majority of income-tax payers (95 per cent) face a marginal tax rate of 34 per cent (25 per cent income tax, combined with 9 per cent national insurance contributions). However, the loss of family credit and housing benefit ensures that some poor working families face a marginal tax rate of three times this level. 'For a full-time working family paying income tax and national insurance contributions, and receiving income-related benefits, an extra £1 of gross earnings can lead to an increase in income tax of 25p, a 9p increase in national insurance contributions, a 46p reduction in family credit, and a 17p reduction in Housing Benefit – a total of 97p' (*Hansard*, 28 July 1988, col. 509). While it is correct, therefore, for the Government to claim that poor families are not theoretically faced with marginal tax rates in excess of 100 per cent, it is clear that low-income families as a group face marginal tax rates of double, and sometimes treble, what the majority of the population pays. The Treasury and Civil Service Committee ended its deliberations on the poverty trap by recording: 'It is clear from the foregoing that the extreme version of the poverty trap, so called – i.e. the problem of working families facing a marginal rate of 100% – is only the tip of an iceberg' (p. 23).

'Why Work?' Syndrome

It is also the tip of the iceberg in another sense, for this complex of wage levels and tax rates that we have been examining also leads to another obstacle for those on welfare being able to improve themselves by taking a job, even if one is available. Ralph Howell was the first politician to draw attention to the narrowness of the gap between the income of many low-wage earners when in work, and their benefit entitlement when they were without a job. (See his *Low Pay and Taxation*, Low Pay Paper, no. 8, p. 20, LPU, 1976.)

The ratio of a person's net income when in work compared to their income on benefit is measured by what is called the 'replacement ratio'. If a person's replacement ratio is high, it means that their income from benefit is near to their net income from work. On the other hand, if the replacement ratio is low, this denotes that benefit income is considerably below that which a person would receive when in work.

Since 1979, the Government has taken three measures to lower the replacement ratio – that is, to increase the gap between a person's income when in work compared with when he or she is drawing the dole. The earnings-related supplement, paid to eligible claimants during the first six months of unemployment, has been abolished; unemployment pay is now taxable; and tax rebates are not now paid immediately to those losing their jobs. Other factors also have an effect on the level of the replacement rate, for example wage increases and the movement of rent and rates, together with benefit levels. How these measures have affected the replacement rates can be seen in table 14.2.

Table 14.2　*Replacement rates for the working population, 1978, 1985–1986*

| Working households with replacement rates below (%) | Percentages of all working households | | | |
| | November 1978 | | 1985–6 | |
	Short-term	Long-term	Short-term	Long-term
40	2	10	10	11
50	7	31	24	25
60	21	56	44	46
70	43	75	68	70
80	65	88	87	89
90	82	94	96	97
100	92	97	99	99
110	97	98	100	100
Average rate	74	60	62	61

Source　Institute of Fiscal Studies.

Between November 1978 and November 1986, short-term replacement rates have fallen; for example, whereas 65 per cent of claimants had an income below 80 per cent of their normal earnings in 1978, this had risen to 87 per cent of claimants in 1986. So, too, have long-term rates, but not to such a significant degree. This has led a number of commentators to argue that the unemployment trap is now of little importance to the real world. Using the data in the table, an argument is advanced that, whereas 21 per cent of working families had a short-term replacement rate of up to 60 per cent of their normal earnings in 1978, by 1985–6 this had risen to about 44 per cent of families.

Despite the reassuring noises made by the Government, the poverty and unemployment traps play an all too real and oppressive role in the lives of those on low incomes. It is unfair, to say the least, in a country that increasingly believes that incentives should be the dominant motive force, that the interaction of taxation rates and benefit eligibility levels should preclude the least privileged from being able to improve their own lot. More importantly, this interaction is now playing a crucial part in excluding the underclass from the mainstream of society. While the poverty trap affects very large numbers of workers – including some who are part of the underclass – the unemployment trap is one that particularly operates against this group, especially those at its margin. One way open to the individual to beat these two traps is to make dishonest returns to the tax office, the benefit office, or both. Participation in the black economy may produce substantial short-term gains for the individual concerned, but these gains have to be offset against the 'rights of citizenship' that go with a complete national insurance contributions record. Such exclusion from citizenship is again the mark of the underclass. Reforming the tax system in order to reduce sharply the standard rate of tax is considered in Part IV.

Summary

Large numbers of people in Britain are reduced to subsisting on a low income once they are unable to work. To prevent these people becoming poor, the post-war welfare reforms enacted a series of national insurance benefits to cover those periods when people were excluded from the labour market – in old age, during sickness or unemployment. These benefits, however, were never paid at a generous enough level to prevent many of those without work from having to resort also to means-tested assistance. While the number of people drawing such assistance grew steadily during the post-war period, the size of this group has exploded since 1979. So, while the Government claims that it is targeting help on those in greatest need, it is simultaneously increasing the numbers caught, in the Government's terminology, in a 'dependency culture'. This fundamental contradiction, between wanting to target help – which means increasing the numbers on means-tested assistance – and breaking the dependency culture, is one that has thwarted the whole of the Government's welfare and tax policies. While no working poor families are now subjected to 100 per cent marginal tax rates, large numbers of them face the combined effect of tax and loss of means-tested benefits, which withdraws over three-quarters of any increased income they earn. Similarly, because of the loss of full housing benefit once a person moves off income support, a large number of unemployed families face what has been called an unemployment trap. While the numbers affected by these disincentives are far greater than the membership of the underclass, the underclass is the most severely affected. The other 'fixing' agents, which have been described in this chapter, act to create a catch-22 situation. They prevent most of the underclass from being able to free themselves from welfare dependency. But it is only with the chance of full-time work that this group can build up its rights to social insurance benefits, which prevents any further misfortune resulting in an automatic relegation to dependency on means-tested assistance. Reforms aimed at refashioning the welfare state, so that it acts as a floor on which the underclass can build by their own efforts, rather than a ceiling through which it is impossible for them to pass, are considered in Part IV.

15

Capital Divisions

There are currently a number of changes at work that are likely to prevent the poor from acquiring capital assets. These same forces will also further distance the underclass from the vast majority of the population, many of whom now have a stake in what is called 'people's capitalism'. Paradoxically, the moves to widen the number of people holding capital assets is being accompanied by a determined attempt to reverse the sixty-year-old trend towards greater equality of wealth. Recent fiscal changes affecting the ownership of wealth have been considered in Part II. In this chapter, the discussion is concerned with how the Government's privatization measures, together with the sale of council houses and the change in the relative prices of different forms of capital assets, interact to isolate still further the underclass.

Relative Values

Two moves are in progress that are likely to have reversed the slow move towards equality in the ownership of wealth. First, industrial wealth, signified in the form of stocks and shares, has increased rapidly in value, despite recent fluctuations on the stock market. This change has, however, been accompanied by a rise in home ownership and an explosion in house prices, which has been the second force at work affecting the distribution of wealth. Much of the owner-occupation sector represents a recent addition to national wealth; from 26.6 per cent in 1957 to 36.5 per cent of all wealth by 1985 – a 37 per cent increase in thirty years (Sam Brittan, 'Keeping an eye on the national wealth', *Financial Times*, 16 July 1987), and this wealth has been much more equitably spread than has industrial wealth. So, while the stock market boom has played a crucial part in entrenching the wealth position of those who own most, the spread of owner-occupation, coupled with the rapid rise in house prices, has been largely responsible for extending the scope of capital ownership to well over 60 per cent of the population. This latter move was accelerated by Mrs Thatcher's policy of council house sales.

With the spread of home ownership, a process that began in earnest during the inter-war years and has accelerated since the 1960s, the passing on of the family home will become an increasingly important aspect of defining who owns what, and confirming the advantages enjoyed by some groups of the population. The inheritance factor is already taking two forms. There is the sale of the family home by grandparents and the transfer of what are often quite large sums of capital to grandchildren in the form of a down payment on a new home. Alternatively, these assets are left untouched, and are inherited by the grandparents' children. Practically all of this latter group are the owners of their own home. Inheritance therefore benefits those who already possess substantial capital assets.

A similar trend is also developing whereby parents sell their home when their children have established an independent existence. Trading in for a smaller house or flat again releases considerable capital, which is often shared with the offspring. Without such a capital gift, it is now impossible for many young people to make a first-time purchase in most areas of London and the South-East. The rise in house prices, which has recently done so much to increase the capital owned by a sizeable group of the population, has made it increasingly difficult for other people, and particularly those whose parents are poorer and who do not own a house, to join the ranks of the upwardly mobile, capital-accumulating home-owners. The market has well and truly raised the drawbridge against any advance by the less privileged. The only means of advance now is for those able to buy the council house in which they live.

Council House Sales

The sale of council houses has also had an important effect on the distribution of wealth, increasing the amount of wealth in the possession of part of the working class. But the way these sales have been conducted has simultaneously given rise to housing ghettos, along the lines of those in North American cities. The reason for this, not surprisingly, is that the sale of the better properties, and the partial freezing of capital derived from such sales, has resulted in the continued decline, in both quality and quantity, of the remaining housing stock.

The sale of council houses has taken place against the background of an allocation policy that has done much to lay the basis of the emergence of ghettos. Historically, the vast majority of housing departments screened their tenants, putting the 'better class of person', as many housing officers described them, onto the best estates, while ensuring that the poorest tenants were housed in sink areas. It has been this policy of screening tenants over the decades before the main sale of council houses was pushed through by the Government that has resulted in the buying of houses largely on the best estates, and has helped to reinforce the emergence of the ghetto in many areas of Britain.

Failure to improve the condition of the remaining housing stock has also played an important part in the rise of ghetto conditions. A report by the Royal Institute of British Architects in 1985 drew attention to the very poor physical condition of much of the remaining stock in the public sector (*Decaying Britain*, Royal Institute of British Architects, 1985). After a survey of 140 local authorities, the RIBA concluded that the total backlog of repairs and maintainance work to the public sector housing stock was in excess of £10 billion. An even larger problem has been cited in a Department of Environment inquiry into the condition of local authority housing in England. Carried out in 1985, the inquiry found that 3.8 million dwellings, or 84 per cent of the stock, were in need of expenditure totalling £18.8 billion (*An Inquiry into the Condition of Local Authority Housing Stock in England*, DOE, 1988).

The housing conditions of Britain's underclass, who are now largely housed in what remains of the council sector, were described by the report of the Archbishop's Commission, *Faith in the City* (Church House Publishing, 1985), in the following graphic terms. The Commission reported that their visits to the inner and outer areas of the main conurbations convinced them that it is now the large housing estates in the inner ring, or on the fringes of the city, that present the most pressing urban problems in the mid-1980s.

Huge impersonal housing estates, many post-war, can be found in all our cities. They are often spoken of as being 'microchrome' – that is, drab, dreary, depressing, with no vitality, colour or beauty. Many outer estates are nothing less than the architect-designed, system-built slums of our post-war era. They suffer from poor design, defects in construction, poor upkeep of public areas, no 'double-defensible space'; with packs of dogs roaming about, filth in the stair wells, one or two shuttered shops, the main shopping centres a 20-minute expensive bus journey away. Unemployment rates are typically 30–40 per cent and rising. Bored, out-of-work young people turn to vandalism, drugs and crime, and the spiral is given a further twist.   (p. 176)

Unemployment on the estates themselves is much higher than the average for the surrounding areas. The Commissioners, for example, visited the Bidston area of Birkenhead, which has a 48 per cent male unemployment rate: 'but within this [area], there are parts of the Ford Estate . . . where we had evidence that 80 per cent were out of work' (p. 199).

The ghetto effect of these areas was plainly stated in the Commissioners' report.

It is not simply that these areas suffer from deprivation and poverty, but there is a danger of many outer estates, in particular, becoming areas which have a quite different social and economic system, operating almost at subsistence level, depending entirely on the public sector, where the opportunities for improvement either through self-help or through outside intervention are minimal.   (p. 175)

The issue of local economies being spun into what becomes a self-perpetuating decline has been highlighted in a recent report from the Centre for Environmental Studies (*Outer Estates in Britain*, CES Paper, 1984). The findings of this report on four inner-city areas in Liverpool, Glasgow, Hull and Middlesborough are essential to any record of an emerging underclass in Britain.

Reporting on the decade of change following the 1971 Census, the CES found: first, in those areas under consideration, there has been a population decline of 20 per cent, whereas the population at large has grown. The balance of this reduced population has changed dramatically: the proportion of under-fives has dropped by a quarter, and the numbers of those at school leaving age by just under a quarter, giving an overall decline of 15 per cent in the population aged under fifteen. In marked contrast to this fall amongst younger age groups, the number of retired people had increased by 39 per cent. Second, the report concluded that unemployment in these estates had almost doubled during the intervening decade, and, while the proportion of women working in the area remained roughly stable, the national trend revealed a substantial rise.

It has been demonstrated that the dominance of unemployment in these outer estates has had a growing impact on the relative decline in income in each of these areas. This is because benefits are below, and sometimes substantially below, current wage levels. Further, this growing number on welfare have seen their income since 1979 increase only marginally above the rise in prices, while earnings have risen substantially above the rate of inflation.

Overall, the Census data suggest not only that the standard of living for those already on state benefits in 1971 has fallen further behind, 'but that many more of the residents have become dependent upon benefits and have so little disposable income as to be unable to participate in the consumer society at all' (p. 17).

The CES went on to assert that:

It could be that the outer estates are approaching some kind of basic 'subsistence' level, where disposable income has reached such a low level that future increases in unemployment will begin to have a smaller effect in reducing local incomes per head, simply because so many people are already dependent on state benefits. (p. 17)

The isolating effect for whole areas caused by a fall in income to subsistence level is explained in the CES report in the following way.

The absence of significant disposable income in the community would mean that it would be difficult for new economic activity to develop, there being no local income to compete for. It would lead to lack of competition in local retailing and an increasing reliance on basic 'no frills' stores, selling only a restricted range of products. The fact that fewer people were participating in the 'cash' economy, since more and more were having their rent, bills etc. paid directly by one public agency to another would also tend to debilitate the private sector, and may have serious social repercussions by producing a culture of dependence, alienation and apathy. (p. 18)

Share Capital

Current moves to encourage wider share ownership will again distance the underclass from higher-income groups. While the efforts of the

Government's privatization proposals have been weighted towards the small investor, there is little evidence that the poor have been beneficiaries. True, the number of shareholders has increased, from 2 million in 1979 to an estimated 7 million in 1987. The latter figure allows for those who played the market: those who, having bought shares as a result of one or more privatizations, sold them in order to realize a quick capital gain. However, as the Stock Exchange itself observed: 'Shareholders currently have an "up market" profile, [with] 42 per cent of them falling into social grades A or B.... Within the adult population as a whole, only 17 per cent fall into these two social grades' (*The Changing Face of Share Ownership*, Stock Exchange, 1986, p. 4).

In the case of working-class families who have bought shares – and this group in no way overlaps with the underclass – such purchases are likely to be small in value. The Stock Exchange does not provide a class distribution according to size of holdings, yet the 23 per cent of shareholders who own stock valued at less than £500 are unlikely to be found at the upper end of the income scale. Similarly, for many lower-income groups, the spread of companies in which they have shares will be very limited. One survey found that over half of all shareholders (4.1 million) owned stock in only one company (Dewe Rogerston, report in the *Financial Times*, 13 December 1986).

A further force for polarization appears to be at work. A poll, specially commissioned by London Weekend Television, examined the attitudes of different age groups to wealth distribution ('The rich in Britain', *New Society*, 22 August 1986). The elderly, who have already lived most of their politically active lives, were more favourably inclined to redistribution than were the younger people in the sample. The formative years of many of the elderly who were surveyed was a time of popular demand for greater equality. Today, many young people, with most of their voting years ahead of them, are more likely than before to feel that they can make it alone. The political challenge for those on the left is how to meet this self-assertiveness, which is clearly linked to self-fulfilment, while at the same time building support for policies that favour those on low incomes and the underclass.

Summary

Paradoxically, 'people's capitalism' has been ushered in at a time when the long-term trend towards a greater equality in wealth may have been reversed, and in a manner that has firmly excluded the poorest from acquiring capital assets themselves. Despite the fact that the rich have become considerably richer in the recent past, due largely to the relative rise in the value of industrial capital, combined with an array of favourable tax changes, large numbers of other citizens are in the process of acquiring the ownership of their own homes, considerable pension rights and a small portfolio of shares. This policy has not, however, become universal, and the sale of council houses in particular has been conducted in a way that is creating ghetto areas of very poor public housing, populated largely by the very old, the unemployed and single mothers on welfare. This underclass has been isolated further by a crucial change in the political climate. Young people are more likely than older voters to be against egalitarian measures favouring those who have yet to gain a capital stake in our society. This change in attitudes plays a crucial part in the development of a drawbridge mentality, which is replacing the more collective outlook of previous decades.

16

Completing the Cycle of Deprivation

Whereas until now we have been considering changes that are forming an underclass, we now turn to examine a reform already enacted that will ensure that the underclass, and other vulnerable groups, continue to be the least privileged in old age. This section begins by looking at the changing fate of old people during the past century as they have retired. It considers the various pension reforms aimed at breaking the link between poverty and old age, and concludes by examining how the Thatcher Government's scaling down of SERPS (the State Earnings-Related Pension Scheme) will ensure that today's underclass take their poverty into old age.

Old Age and Poverty

As was seen in Part I, the link between poverty and old age has changed over time. When Seebohm Rowntree carried out his first study of poverty in York in 1899, he found that around 1 per cent of the poor were old people, largely because most working-class people worked until they died, or were incarcerated in the workhouse. By 1936, the year of Rowntree's second survey in York, 15 per cent of the poor were found to be old people, but this was still adjudged to be a far less significant cause of poverty than unemployment or low wages. Rowntree carried out his third survey of living standards in York in 1951. This recorded a dramatic decline in the total number of poor, largely due to the implementation of the Beveridge Report in 1948. However, of the significantly reduced number who were found to be poor, 68 per cent were pensioners (table 5.1 of A. B. Atkinson, 'Low pay and the cycle of poverty', in *Low Pay*, ed. Frank Field, Arrow

Books, London, 1973). Ironically, the number of old people who were poor would have been greater but for the action of the Attlee Government. The Beveridge Report advocated the payment of old-age pensions on an actuarial basis, which would have meant the building up of contributions over a twenty-year period. The Labour Government was not prepared to let those who were pensioners at the time die in poverty, while awaiting the gradual implementation of a new scheme. It therefore ruled that the new pensions should be paid to existing pensioners, but at a value below that advocated by Beveridge. This move had a dramatic effect on the income of pensioners in 1948, but flawed the Beveridge scheme in the long run by ensuring that many pensioners would have to continue resorting to means-tested benefits. (For further details see chapter 4, 'What went wrong?', of *Freedom and Wealth in a Socialist Future*, Frank Field, Constable, London, 1987.)

Throughout the 1960s, a number of surveys that highlighted the growing problem of low income and poverty amongst pensioners were carried out. (See, for example, P. Townsend and D. Wedderburn, *The Aged and the Welfare State*, Bell, London, 1965, pp. 125–6.) These findings were confirmed by two official surveys. In the report of the Committee of Inquiry into the *Impact of Rates on Households*, it was stated that 900,000 old people, living in 800,000 households, had incomes at, or below, the official poverty line (Cmnd. 2582, HMSO, 1965). Another report, by the Ministry of Pensions and National Insurance, provided statistics revealing the number of old-age pensioners who had no other income, apart from their old-age pension or supplementary benefit: 1 in 9 married couples, 1 in 4 single men, and 1 in 3 single women had no additional income whatsoever. In total, 1 in 5 old people were dependent upon state benefit for their sole income (*Financial and other Circumstances of Retired Pensioners*, HMSO, 1967, p. 11).

Since these reports on the aged poor were first published in the 1960s, two changes have occurred that have radically changed the financial position of many of those who have retired. As illustrated in Part I, there has been a growth in occupational pension schemes. In addition, there have been major reforms in state provisions for pensioners. Both of these changes are of sufficient importance to warrant individual consideration.

The General Household Survey collected information on occupational pension schemes in its 1975, 1979 and 1983 surveys (reported in

GHS 1983, HMSO, 1985). These showed an increase, between 1975 and 1979, in the proportions of both men and women who are members of occupational pension schemes, rising from 63 per cent to 68 per cent for the former, and from 47 per cent to 55 per cent for the latter. However, the proportion of men covered by occupational pension schemes had fallen slightly by 1983 to 66 per cent, while the proportion of women in schemes remained constant (table 7.42).

Coverage by occupational pension schemes is not, however, evenly distributed amongst all social classes. Membership is consistently higher in the non-manual socio-economic groups. There is also a significant difference in membership between full- and part-time workers. In 1983, for example, men working full time were three times more likely to be covered than were men working part time. The difference was even more marked among women, where women working full time were four times more likely to belong to such a scheme than those in part-time work. Part-time workers were more likely to work for an employer who did not offer an occupational pension scheme. Moreover, 'even where there was a scheme, they [i.e. part-time workers] were less likely than full-time workers to belong' (p. 99).

This finding is significant in itself, but it becomes even more so when matched against the changes in the labour market already described, where part-time working is increasingly important, and not only for women.

There is an increasing correlation between membership of an occupational scheme and level of earnings: the higher the level of earnings, the greater the chances of being a member of such a scheme. Among full-time male workers, fewer than 20 per cent of those with gross earnings of £75.00 a week or less were covered by a current employer's scheme, compared with 80 per cent of those with gross weekly earnings of more than £150. An equally strong income gradient exists for female workers (p. 100).

Information relating to the size of pensions derived from occupational schemes is provided by the Government Actuary Department (GAD). The latest report is for 1983, and it demonstrates that the average weekly pension paid to men covered by a public occupational pension scheme was £44; the corresponding figure for those in a private occupational scheme was £30. The respective figures for retired women in 1983 were £35 and £15 (table 3.3, *Occupational Pension Schemes, 1983*, GAD, HMSO, 1986).

This information indicates that occupational schemes provide an important coverage for many pensioners. The coverage of these schemes is, however, incomplete, and those least likely to enjoy coverage are those on the lowest incomes. Almost half of all workers are still left without occupational coverage, and, for some of those who do gain an occupational pension, the value is often small (*Occupational Pension Schemes, 1983*, table 3.3). Not surprisingly, the state has also interested itself in providing additional pension coverage.

The first attempt at building an earnings-related element into the flat-rate retirement pension came in 1958. Known as the Boyd–Carpenter scheme, employees made graduated contributions towards a graduated pension. The scheme was modest, so modest in fact that a number of experts were quick to point out that, even when the scheme was fully mature, it would still provide inadequate pensions to guarantee most beneficiaries, without any pension other than the state retirement pension, an income above the official poverty line. (See A. B. Atkinson, *Poverty in Britain and the Reform of Social Security*, Cambridge University Press, Cambridge, 1969, pp. 52–4.)

In the 1966–70 Parliament, the Labour Government introduced the most ambitious of state pension schemes. Known as the Crossman scheme, it failed to gain parliamentary approval before the 1970 election. After 1974, the Labour Government introduced a measure known as the State Earnings-related Pension Scheme, or SERPS for short. This came into effect in 1975, and held out the prospect that, once full pensions became payable under the terms of the new scheme, no qualifying pensioner would face poverty in old age.

The Thatcher Government initially decided to abolish SERPS on the basis that the country could not afford it, a view contested by the Government Actuary's report on the proposed changes (*Report by the Government Actuary on the Financial Effects of the Bill on the National Insurance Fund*, Cmnd. 9711, HMSO, 1986). Under pressure, not least from some of the Government's own back-benchers and the pension industry, the Government buckled, and introduced a more 'modest' reform. The original Conservative proposal had been to unload all secondary or graduated pensions on to the private sector. The private sector, however, had no intention of extending coverage to those who could offer it little or no return on their balance sheet. The 'compromise' approved by Parliament made a two-pronged attack on the state scheme. In the first place, the pension being offered was roughly halved in value. Further, instead of taking the average of the twenty best years' earnings after 1978, SERPS will now take an average earnings of all years worked. The maximum pension will now be 20 per cent, rather than 25 per cent of average pensionable earnings. The pension offered to widows has been cut in half.

The second attack on SERPS comes in the form of incentives given for contracting out. Employers have always been able to contract out their workers from the scheme if they offered an acceptable alternative. Now, individual workers will be able to leave the state scheme even if they do not belong to a recognized scheme. A minimum contribution, equal to a part of the national insurance contributions paid by both employees and their employers, will be invested in a pension plan, and for this the employees will gain tax relief on their national insurance contributions. In addition, until April 1993, a further 2 per cent subsidy based on earnings will be paid. Joanna Slaughter of the *Observer*, estimates that a backdated personal pension plan of 9.05 per cent of band earnings is there for the asking at *no cost to the employee* (*Observer*, 26 June 1986). The cost is instead being borne by taxpayers and poorer workers who will remain in SERPS. The major significance of the Government's changes is highlighted by the fact that, whereas SERPS held out the prospect of guaranteeing every pensioner an income above the supplementary pension level, no Government minister had felt able to give a similar guarantee for the Thatcher pension reform.

The first part of this chapter detailed the significant rise in both the real and the relative income of pensioners. But this analysis gave average figures, and combined data covering pensioners dependent on state benefits alone, as well as those who were also drawing occupational pensions. The fate of these two groups is now very different.

Up to 1980, the increase in real income for pensioners was mainly accounted for by increases in the basic pension and other social security payments. As a result, all pensioners gained a 20 per cent increase in their basic old-age pensions, but, for obvious reasons, poorer pensioners experienced the greatest percentage increase in their real pensions. Since 1980, the position has been reversed, with the increase in real income of pensioners being accounted for by a substantial real increase in occupational pensions. During the last nine years, it has been richer pensioners who have been the main beneficiaries of the real increase in the value of pensions.

Although the Government has maintained the real value of the retirement pensions, its breaking of the link between state pensions and earnings (see Part II) is beginning to have a devastating effect on the relative income of the poorest pensioners. Under the last Labour Government, state pensions rose by 20 per cent in real terms. Under this Government, the rise has been a little over 2 per cent. The value of the basic pension stood at 21 per cent as measured against average earnings in 1979. By the end of this century, the estimate is that it will have dropped to around 15 per cent.

This fall in value, plus the scaling down of SERPS, will have a dramatic effect on pensioners' incomes by the end of the century. A sixteen year old beginning work in a low-paid job in 1988 would have been entitled to a pension of £128 per week on retirement in 2037 when average earnings will be £411 a week. Under the new rules this same person can expect a pension of half the original amount: £64 per week, or one-eighth of average earnings.

If the Government's approach continues unamended, and if there is no major industrial slump affecting the returns from investments, the living standards of pensioners dependent on occupational sources of income and savings are likely to move even further away from those mainly dependent on state benefits, who will get poorer relative both to other pensioners and to the rest of the community. On present policies, according to Jeremy Lawrence, we 'risk creating a pensioner underclass that the new private sources of income cannot reach' (*New Society*, 5 June 1987; the data for the last three paragraphs is drawn from the same source).

Summary

People have always been more vulnerable in old age. Not only does their health become more problematic, but their income drops – at least in the case of those without substantial private means. Despite being the aim of many state pension schemes, the breaking of the link between old age and low income was a real possibility with SERPS. The effectiveness of this measure has now been neutralized, in order to boost private welfare. Occupational pensions are undoubtedly delivering the goods for those people who are members. But the success of these schemes is heavily dependent on the recent improvement in the rate of return of private investment, and, moreover, the coverage provided by private schemes is incomplete. Since 1979, those dependent on state pensions alone have seen their income fall way behind those who had two or more pensions. The inequality in life chances has therefore intentionally been reinforced in old age.

CONCLUSION

Despite the existence of a welfare state, crucial differences in life chances have remained as wide as ever in post-war Britain. That was the situation before the election of Mrs Thatcher's first government in 1979, which openly campaigned on the need to make society more unequal. Under the objective of letting 'the children grow tall', that is precisely what the Government has achieved with respect to the distribution of income and wealth, and in the provision of state and private welfare. This is not to say that the Government has not also been pursuing other policies, such as the wider spread of home ownership, that have been beneficial to many working-class people, but the approach has been implemented in a way that has isolated the underclass still further. While the underclass in this country is held firmly in place by unemployment, a number of other trends, such as tax and benefit disincentives, and structural changes in the job market, are operating to support the downward kick unemployment has on the living standards of this group. The range of policies needed to counter the root causes that have given rise to the underclass and keep it firmly in place at the bottom of the social hierarchy are examined in Part IV.

Part IV

Freeing the Underclass

17

A National Balance Sheet

A young Muscovite worker was asked what difference *perestroika* was making to his life. He replied with a single word – 'hope'. *Perestroika* on the left in British politics needs to have an even higher objective than this single, noble aim. To be able to turn dreams into reality requires power. Power requires a wider appeal than that to mere sectional interest. To gain a wide appeal needs: first, a well thought-out programme; second, an excitement of both self-interest and altruism; and third, a party running its own affairs in such a way that the electorate will trust it in managing the nation's business. By necessity, this part of the book can only deal with some of these requirements, and it begins by discussing the grounds on which a wide appeal can be made to counter the existence of an underclass. The main part, however, is concerned with detailing a political programme that makes a pitch both for self-interest as well as a concern for others.

The Record

Since 1979, the Government has unleashed what amounts to a permanent revolution with one central theme dominating the Prime Minister's programme (for a fuller record of Mrs Thatcher's stewardship, see Peter Jenkins, *Mrs Thatcher's Revolution*, Jonathan Cape, London, 1987). During much of the post-war period, commentators had drawn attention not only to Britain's relative economic decline, but also to the dangers of the country entering a period of absolute decline. The Government's programme has been aimed at preventing this scenario. Beginning with the entries on the plus side, how does the national balance sheet look in meeting this objective?

One undoubted plus has been the significant improvement in the performance of Britain's economy. The Introduction gave details of Britain's growth rate during this century. Compared with most of Europe and Japan, but surprisingly not with the United States, Britain has historically had a low rate of economic growth. During the inter-war years, the average rate of growth was 1.2 per cent. During the period of rebuilding the economy after World War Two, the growth rate averaged only 1.4 per cent. If the first two years of the Thatcher Government are excluded – when the Government managed to achieve a negative rate of growth – the British economy has grown at an average rate of 3 per cent. During 1988, the rate of growth was around 7 per cent, a rate that cannot be sustained and will cause severe 're-entry' problems as the Government tries to get the economy back to a realistic long-term rate of performance.

Matching the Government's economic achievement has been its attempts to change the way Britons collectively think about work. R. H. Tawney observed that the workman's philosophy was the same as his masters: 'get as much and give as little as possible'. This same attitude has underlain much of the industrial conflict during this century, and was to Tawney, and others, a 'disgrace even it was explicable in terms of the evils sown and ripened in a 150 years of capitalist morality' (see Norman Dennis and A. H. Halsey, *English Ethical Socialism*, Clarendon Press, Oxford, 1988, p. 163). The rottenness of this short-sighted attitude, which is shown by both sides of industry, has begun to change, and is being replaced by a growing realization that a great trading nation is not owed a living by the rest of the world; rather, it has to earn it.

Linked with this attitudinal change has been a third major plus – the Government's reform of trade unions. On this, as on other issues, the outcome of the Government actions has been good, even if its motives for seeking the reforms are suspect. Certainly, the Prime Minister presents this programme as part of her detestation of socialism in particular, and the labour movement in general. But whatever the motives, the Government's twin aims of handing back the control of unions to the individual members, and ensuring that trade unions act within bounds set by a democratic state, are ones that should have been promoted by the left. Yet in tackling the nastier aspects to be seen in British trade unionism by the late 1970s, the Government itself has adopted an equally obnoxious bullying style that is characteristic of much of its activities. Indeed, this attitude itself marks the transition of the plus side of the national balance sheet since 1979, onto the debit side of the account.

Here, three items in particular need to be recorded. First, the advent of mass unemployment. The number of people without work rose more rapidly, and to a higher level in the two years following 1979 than at any other time during the post-war period. In its defence, the Government pleads mitigating circumstances. Time after time, ministers have tried to shift the blame for rising unemployment to the down-turn in the world economy. Clearly, this has played a role, but *The Report of the House of Lords Select Committee on Overseas Trade* (HMSO, 1985, pp. 238–41) concluded that the responsibility for at least half of the increase in unemployment since 1979 is laid directly at the Government's door. The significant rise in the value of the pound from 1979 played a major part in crippling Britain's export performance, while making imports that much cheaper. This miscalculation of letting the value of sterling appreciate led not so much to a slim-down of manufacturing industry but to the closure of whole plants. It is very difficult to 'rebuild' Britain's competitiveness if the basis for that rebuilding are derelict industrial estates waiting to be grassed over with the help of Government landscaping grants. Whatever the reasons for inaction, rising unemployment has not been uniformly spread over the entire population, but instead has struck hardest at these who are already the most vulnerable.

A similar, selective approach has characterized the way the Government has attempted to create an incentive-based culture. On the income side, this aim has been pursued by cutting the rates of tax. While this has without doubt provided an incentive for those on higher earnings, the record is more suspect when it comes to those on average earnings. The standard rate of tax has been reduced from 33p to 25p in the pound. But in the same period the Government has increased the rate of national insurance contributions from 6.5 to 9 per cent, and, because these rates start at a lower threshold than taxation, the net effect has been to mitigate the changes in income tax. Moreover, both directly through its fiscal policy, and indirectly by affecting the distribution of market income, the Government has ensured that the very poorest have been excluded from any significant share in the exceptional rise in the nation's wealth.

The selectivity of the Government's approach is again illuminated by once again comparing the treatment handed out to those at the bottom of the social hierarchy, where the Government has launched a determined attack on what it calls the 'dependency culture'. The Government's thinking on this issue is confused. The largest part of the current welfare budget is paid out on national insurance benefits – such as old-age pensions and unemployment pay. People are only entitled to these benefits if they have paid the requisite number of contributions. Lessening the attractiveness of these benefits, for which people have directly paid contributions, in the hope of boosting the provision of private welfare, for which people will also have to make contributions, hardly amounts to a clear strategy to reduce welfare dependency. It merely shifts dependency, if that is an appropriate term, from the public to the private sector.

Even less clearly struck has been the Government's attempt to reduce dependency on means-tested welfare. By a whole series of moves, which were discussed in detail in Part II, the Government has made this form of welfare far less attractive – both in the level of payment, and the terms under which it can be obtained. But at the same time, because of the Government's policy of disenfranchising people from entitlement to national insurance benefits, and reducing the income of those already on low incomes, it has significantly increased the numbers claiming means-tested assistance, or, as it prefers to say, targeted help on those in greatest need. However, because benefit is withdrawn as income rises, means-tested benefits often confront claimants with a marginal tax rate in excess of 80 per cent on any additional income. This approach therefore builds a ceiling over the heads of those on low incomes, making it impossible for them to break free.

The distribution of wealth is important because one aim of the radical left should be to ensure that people draw an income from work, welfare and wealth. It is, after all, an approach that has served the rich rather well and will continue to do so, given the sweeping changes that have been made to wealth taxation. The Chancellor recently summed up his own achievements on this front by observing 'I have lightened the tax on inheritance very considerably, both by cutting the rates, and by granting exemptions for lifetime transfers' (interview with Bruce Anderson, *Sunday Telegraph*, 9 October 1988).

While making it easier for people to build up considerable capital assets, and to pass these on intact, the Government has taken a number of measures that have allowed many people to acquire capital assets for the first time. The sale of council housing, and the privatization floatations are cases in point. Yet here, as on the income front, the same pattern emerges. Large numbers of people have gained the advantages of acquiring different forms of capital, be they houses or shares. But this policy has been pursued along with changes that have allowed the very rich to increase still further their own wealth holdings, while simultaneously excluding the very poorest from this process. The political significance of this change should not be underestimated. A considerable number of the newly enfranchised capital class now ally their interests with the top echelons of society, rather than help sustain the old political coalition of interests, encompassing as it did much of the working class, and significant parts of the lower-middle and middle class.

It has been the combined effect of these changes – both on income and capital – that has led to such a growing polarization in living standards between different social groups that a new pattern of class inequalities is becoming apparent. For the reasons already given (see Part I) the death rates of infants provide a sensitive indicator of wider socio-economic changes. Taking the period 1979–85, and dividing it into two parts, we find that in the years since 1983 the differences in surviving birth of infants born to parents in social class I, compared to those whose parents are in social classes IV and V, has widened. *Losing Out* maintains that the widening of class differences along a whole front has largely been brought about by the Government's 'success' in redistributing income and wealth towards the haves to the exclusion of the have-nots, and that this widening of class differences is playing a crucial role in the emergence of an underclass in Britain.

The Fate of the Underclass

Other forces have been at work too. The Government's fiscal and welfare changes, and the consequent widening of class differences, have been reinforced by the advent of mass unemployment. It is the combined effect of all these forces, together with the political isolation of the most vulnerable in society, which is leading to a disenfranchisement of one part of the population from full citizenship. It is the loss of a comprehensive approach to citizenship that makes it appropriate to talk in terms of an emerging underclass. Three groups are easy prey to the underclass's recruiting sergeant. These are those who have been unemployed longest, and generally speaking are very young claimants with few skills, or older workers who, by the length of this unemployment, have been de-skilled. A second group is made up of single mothers who are dependent on means-tested welfare into the indefinite future. The third vulnerable group of the population are the very elderly with only a state pension. These three groups share common characteristics which mark them out from the rest of the population, even from many of those who are on low income.

What has been meant by full social and economic membership of the community was developed earlier this century, first with the national insurance reforms of the 1906 Liberal Government, and then with the development of these policies, together with the commitment to full employment of the immediate post-war era. Mass unemployment has led to an exclusion from sharing in the country's prosperity, and thereby in the hope of seeing one's economic position improve, for a significant group of the population. It has also resulted in downward mobility for a significant proportion of the working class. This loss of full participation as a consumer has been reinforced by a whole series of changes limiting eligibility to the national insurance unemployment benefit. Income as of right has been replaced by income conditional on qualifying for means-tested support.

This reversal of universal citizenship with respect to both economic and welfare entitlement is to be accompanied by an assault on a universal political citizenship. The Government intends to change the basis of local authority taxation. A central Government contribution will remain, along with a reformed business rate, but in place of a levy on the value of a person's home, individuals within a house will be required to pay a community charge, more accurately described as a poll tax. The overall effect of this tax will be to redistribute income still further from those on lower incomes to those on higher incomes. The move will favour those people in high-spending authorities who live in expensive, and therefore high-rated property, or who are single-person households, or part of a small household. Those who live in a high-spending authority, inhabit an expensive house and are part of a small household will find themselves at a triple advantage.

Originally, the Government's intention was to keep the compiling of the electoral register separate from the poll tax register. However, recent developments suggest that this 'Chinese wall' will be breached, and this suspicion has long been voiced by many poorer people. One way of preparing to evade the poll tax is therefore to disappear from the electoral roll. The cost of this move is high in terms of political citizenship, for without an entry on the electoral register, a person is unable to vote. By this means, the Government is accompanying its move away from full citizenship on economic and welfare fronts to a curtailment in the political domain. We now turn to consider why a counter-strategy should be mounted against this loss of a universal citizenship.

Why Bother?

In the article referred to in the Introduction, Ralf Dahrendorf maintains that the underclass is not a revolutionary threat to political stability, and that accommodating political change will not be induced by this argument. Desperately deprived groups do not organize to bring about the downfall of a political system. Indeed, other evidence cited in the Introduction suggests that many of the underclass, young and old alike, have strong conservative instincts when it comes to politics. Any revolutionary aspirations of the younger members are centred on gaining work and admittance to the mainstream of ordinary life.

This does not mean that the younger members of the underclass pose no threat to public order. There have been a number of large-scale inner-city riots in recent years. Most liberals, if asked in 1979 what would be the effect of a rise in unemployment to well over 3 million would have predicted that democratic government would be made impossible. Even allowing for the surprising restraint that the media has shown in not reporting some instances that local residents would term 'a riot', Britain remains a remarkably peaceful society, if the riot index is the only indicator used. A rather different picture emerges if the subject is broadened to include crime. As Dahrendorf perceptively writes, there 'may not be official "no-go" areas for the police in our cities, but there certainly are such areas for the rest of us'.

Another line of argument put forward by traditional liberals is that an appeal to the better off can be made on the grounds that the existence of the underclass tends to make our society a less civilized one in which to live. Again, I do not believe that enough of the electorate can be persuaded to act on these grounds alone. One of the crucial changes brought about by Mrs Thatcher is the attitude of those who have made it and believe that others can do likewise, or, if they fail to do so, are judged as having not really tried. This 'closed drawbridge' mentality from those who have safely gained access to the good life, or at least a better life, is itself one of the factors that is having a 'ghettoizing' effect on the underclass. With the Thatcher Government, and now to a large extent the Labour Party, appealing to the better off, this trend, if anything, is likely to be reinforced.

A much more dramatic break with the current political tradition is required if progress is to be made in building support for the policies that could spring Britain's underclass from its current position. It is very unlikely that any opposition party will win an election until it convinces the electorate that it has an economic policy which is internally coherent and a defence policy which measures up to its name. Few, if any voters are going to opt for a high-risk economic strategy that could result in a real cut in living standards. But if we assume that such an appeal can be successfully made on the economic front, this strategy needs to be knitted in with a range of other policies that appeal to altruism as well as self-interest. Much of this altruistic appeal can be made in terms of common decency, for this has been the basis on which radical politicians in the past have made their pitch.

Yet it is important not to underestimate the difficulties for politicians wishing to make such an appeal. Generations of Britain's elite have been taught to believe that there are no absolute moral principles. The political effect of this line has been profound. It privatized morality and undermined the status of those verities that should govern both private and public conduct. Above all it held up to ridicule the idea that political decisions should be taken within a moral framework.

The left also has to draw itself out of the mire into which it has been plunged following the 1960s renaissance of Marxist ideas in the Labour movement. The political effect of this development was dramatic. Within a short space of time, Labour's traditional approach based on careful empirical observation of issues was overwhelmed. The contrast between the ethical socialist and a Marxist approach could not be more dramatic. Ethical socialism is essentially a method of 'doing' politics within an agreed moral framework. The Marxist approach is one of fitting political activity within the confines of a given ideology. Ethical socialism, which is at heart a political expression of common decencies, collapsed amazingly quickly in the face of the simple ideological certainties espoused by a new generation of Marxist thinkers and politicians. Three election defeats later, a growing proportion of the left is more sanguine about such an approach. Hence the chance to reassert the old ethical tradition and its appeal. This appeal to common decencies has traditionally been expressed in developing policies that are a direct response to current needs. This is the main purpose of this last part of *Losing Out*, and the proposals are broached in such a way as to appeal to a wider section of the electorate than the underclass alone.

18

Re-establishing Full Employment

Any programme that holds out the hope of eradicating the underclass must be built on the foundation of re-establishing full employment. Full employment will not by itself be sufficient to achieve this objective; it will need to be accompanied by a whole series of other strategies, some of which are detailed in this final section. The move back to full employment, however, must start from the basis that in some areas of the country, and in some parts of the economy, full employment has already been achieved. A full employment programme must therefore be selective – or, to use one of the Government's favourite buzz words, 'targeted'.

It is also necessary to set out a clear idea of what role the public and private sectors can play. It is argued here that the public sector has a crucial part to play in initiating the first moves back to full employment. Only when these have been successfully achieved will the private sector be able to thrive and expand in areas that are currently characterized by high unemployment. There are four major initiatives a Government can undertake.

Relocation of Civil Service Jobs

The first move is to lay the basis of an effective regional policy. In the past, regional policy has largely depended on attracting private-sector firms into areas of high unemployment through a range of subsidies. Initially, this policy has shown signs of success, with some 'footloose' firms moving part of their operations into areas of high unemployment. The crunch has come, however, when the period of subsidy ends, or when the economy has moved into recession. The evidence shows that, when adjusting output during a downturn in the economy, many firms that have taken advantage of regional assistance contract operations at those plants placed in areas that previously had high unemployment choose to close these plants. Additionally, there have been those employers who have moved from site to site, merely to enjoy the subsidies that come from siting 'new' jobs in areas of high unemployment, and have left as soon as the period of the subsidy has come to an end.

An alternative approach is needed. A comprehensive dispersal of Government jobs into those regions with high unemployment could lay the basis for an effective regional policy, and, in so doing, offer the basis for a move back to full employment in all areas. Even after eight years of a government committed to reducing the size of the Civil Service, the number directly employed by the Government in the public sector stands at 585,383 (*Civil Service Statistics*, HMSO 1987, table 3). These jobs are not evenly distributed over the country. In the North-West, for example, those employed by the Civil Service constitute 1.7 per cent of the civilian workforce (ibid.). This compares with 2.2 per cent for the nation as a whole, and 3.3 per cent in the South-West, which has the highest concentration of Civil Service jobs. To bring the North-West up to the UK average would require an extra 15,500 Civil Service jobs there. To match the proportion of the South-West would require an extra 49,500 jobs (House of Commons Library Statistical Section Note, 18 October 1988).

The first move of a Government committed to re-establishing full employment comprehensively would be to initiate a rolling programme of moving Civil Service jobs from areas of high employment, mainly in the South, to those of high unemployment, predominantly in the North. Given modern information technology, it is not necessary for the administrative part of the Civil Service, as opposed to its policy-making sections, to be located in London, within easy distance of its political master. It matters little to the efficient running of the Civil Service where the administrative work of a department is carried out. An evening out of jobs between regions would be the first step in what, in the longer term, should aim to be an almost complete transfer of government jobs from areas of full employment into areas with the highest levels of unemployment. This is an approach that the Department of Social Security has already begun to implement.

The aim of this policy of dispersing Civil Service jobs is not to increase directly the job opportunities of the unemployed in the economic blackspots. The expectation is that many of these Civil Servants would move with their jobs. The primary aim is to underpin the local economy so that it becomes more attractive to an expansion of the private sector. Each of the transferred jobs will result in an additional salary being spent in the local economy. It is this additional purchasing power that will trigger the secondary investment by the private sector. But without the initial pump-priming operation by the Government, there is little or no chance of attracting this secondary wave of employment. Of course, some of those whose jobs are reallocated in the dispersal policy will decide to look for other employment in the locality in which they currently work. These jobs will hopefully be filled by unemployed people in the area into which the jobs are transferred. While this outcome will be a bonus, it is not the main objective of the exercise.

Targeting, Government Purchasing

The second initiative that should be taken by central government is to shape its purchasing policy so that government contracts are increasingly placed in areas of high unemployment. It is very difficult to put a figure on the size of the public procurement budget, owing to the huge range of goods and services that could be considered as falling within it. However, the European Commission has estimated that for most countries this budget accounts for between 10 and 20 per cent of GDP (Evidence to the House of Lords Select Committee on the European Communities, 1987/8 HL 72, p. 17). In Britain, aside from the Ministry of Defence, which is the largest purchaser in central government, the most significant purchasers are as follows: the Department of Transport, spending about £1 billion a year; Her Majesty's Stationary Office, which spends about £250 million a year; the Property Services Agency, servicing public buildings and other property, spends about £1.8 billion a year; the Central Computer and Telecommunications Agency, responsible for all central government information technology advice, organizes everything from multi-million pound computer systems to peripheral services, such as micro-computers, service and maintainance; the National Health Service spends nearly £3.5 billion annually on a wide range of supplies and services through the NHS authorities; and, finally, local authorities buy a very wide range of goods and services.

It is clear that the Government's spending power presents significant opportunities for procurement 'targeted' on areas of high unemployment. There are, of course, limits to such a policy. Significant parts of the procurement budget are already spent in areas of high unemployment, for example warship orders. Moreover, areas of high unemployment do not necessarily have the factories to make the desired goods. Yet there is ample scope in the budget for government departments to place orders on the basis of an overall strategy aimed at raising industrial efficiency over a set time-scale. It is within this overall objective that a targeted procurement policy should be seen, as *part* of a comprehensive regional policy to stimulate local industrial investment. There are other difficulties that will be cited against such a strategy. For example, a commitment to factories in 'favoured' areas would undermine the principle of competitive tendering and, relatedly, such 'favouritism' would run counter to EEC policy. However, these difficulties have not proved insurmountable in other EEC countries, and targeted public procurement would play a useful role in establishing a move back to full employment.

Raising Skill Levels

The third selective measure governments can use to re-establish full employment is to develop a training programme that raises the skills of the unemployed. British workers, even those in employment, possess on average lower skills than workers from major competitor countries. There is therefore a need to raise skill levels both amongst those in work and those seeking work. Under the current system, there is little incentive for firms to increase the skills of their labour force. Indeed, those employers that undertake training programmes stand the risk of having their workers with their newly acquired skills being poached by employers who undertake little or no training. Raising the level of skills amongst British workers is so crucial, not only to any immediate programmme of moving back to full employment, but also to maintaining and improving Britain's long-term performance, that the question of training cannot be left to the free play of market forces.

Here, however, we confront a paradox. It has recently been pointed out that the level of investment in training is substantially above that usually quoted, but that this money is not spent in the most effective way. Employers currently report that most of this sum is eaten up in labour costs (see 'Massive funding survey uncovers £25 bn outlay', *The Times Educational Supplement*, 5 August 1988). The first move in any programme is to gain the commitment of employers – without this no scheme will work. Local and regional training boards should be established and these boards should be employer led. Trade unionists and educationalists should also be members. In addition, each of the training councils should contain political appointees from each of the major parties. Industrial training is too crucial a question for politicians to remain ignorant about the issues involved. Political membership of each of the industrial training boards will therefore act as a training ground for politicians, who will then be able to use this expertise in helping to shape and develop this aspect of the political debate at both the local and national level.

These training boards should have the authority to impose a 'training levy'. The suggestion is that the levy should vary according to the level and effectiveness of the training undertaken by each firm, as judged by the board and the national training agency. Those who undertake little or no training would pay the highest levy. Those whose training programmes reached the standards set by the board would be exempted part of the levy. And those firms that, in addition to the training programme for their own workers, initiate programmes within their companies to train the unemployed would receive a further rebate. A reform suggested below, to introduce a flexible school leaving age so that some fourteen-year-olds can begin to undertake part-time training with part-time work, needs to be seen as part of this overall training programme. Those firms that take on their payroll the early leavers will again either gain a subsidy via a reduction of their training levy, or, if they are already claiming the maximum rebate, the payment of a grant from the training board.

Operating on the Supply Side

Many of the proposals for re-establishing full employment in the aftermath of the 1979–81 recession were aimed at increasing the level of demand in the economy. Now the major emphasis needs to shift to what is called the supply side, and this change in emphasis is the last selective measure the Government should take. The campaign Full Employment UK argues for a four-pronged attack on the supply side that will guarantee the abolition of long-term unemployment. The first step in achieving this objective is to guarantee a place on Employment Training (ET) for everyone who has been out of work for a long period of time. The ET programme was introduced in September 1988. It currently offers on an annual basis up to 600,000 unemployed people an average of six months training and work experience. The proposal is to guarantee a place on ET, or any other training, education, pre-employment course, for those who have been out of work over a set period of time.

Peter Ashby in *Citizenship, Income and Work* (part II, St George's House, Windsor, 1989) accepts that there will be considerable difficulties in phasing in a guaranteed training place for every long-term unemployed person. There were, after all, difficulties in meeting the Government's objective of guaranteeing places on the Youth Training Scheme for every young person not at work or at school. Ashby therefore proposes phasing in the training guarantee, beginning with the very long-term unemployed – and then progressively extending the guarantee to all those in the dole queues for any length of time.

The second proposal is the introduction of a system of adult 'compacts'. One of the more interesting of recent developments has been the initiation by large firms of local compact schemes whereby they, as employers, guarantee to provide employment for young people leaving local YTS schemes, providing the graduates have gained a predetermined qualification. This idea of a compact should be extended to ET graduates, the aim being to encourage as many employers as possible to recruit from among ET leavers with the appropriate qualifications. Ashby writes that the purpose of the adult compacts is simple. It is 'to maximise the number of ET leavers entering the labour market and minimise the number without employment' (p. 9).

The third proposal is for the introduction of a temporary work safety-net. Graduates from ET, or other training and educational courses, should immediately be given another personal needs assessment should they still find themselves without employment. Many people finding themselves in this position would also benefit from spending a few weeks engaged in extensive job search activities as members of a Job Club. The final fall-back position for this group of very hard to place unemployed people should be the offer of a place on a temporary work scheme. These places should be developed by the new Training and Enterprise Councils. The scheme would offer temporary work for up to four days a week, with the other day being set aside for continuing job search.

Since it would be a temporary work programme, and not a training scheme, these 'intermediate workers' would be paid the weekly rate for the job, minus the pay for the day spent searching for an alternative form of employment. The proposal is that the Training and Enterprise Councils should encourage private sector employers, as well as public employers and voluntary bodies, to offer temporary work for unemployed ET workers. The proposals made for guaranteed work by the House of Commons Select Committee on Employment are also relevant to any scheme of providing a bridging mechanism between training on the one hand and permanent employment in the labour market on the other (*Special Employment Measures and the Long-term Unemployed*, House of Commons Paper 99, 1986).

The fourth of Ashby's proposals consists of the introduction of special incentives to employers, both in the private and public sector, to take on to their payrolls those who have failed to find work, even though they have done everything asked of them – are actively seeking work, registered for a job, been a member of a Job Club and been on an ET course. There are three major reasons why employers in the private sector do not increase the numbers on their payrolls. The first relates to the level of demand for the products produced. The second relates to the skill of the workers offering themselves for employment. Linked to this is the third factor, the cost of employing these additional workers, and how this sum matches up to the value of the output achieved by each additional worker. The aim of the training programme outlined earlier is to raise substantially the skills of both those in work and those seeking it. It has to be accepted that, in the short run, it is difficult to raise the skills, and therefore the value of the output of marginal workers (marginal in the sense of their position in competing for work). What can be altered in the short term is the cost of employing new workers, and this can be achieved either by forcing down wages, or by reducing the employer's costs.

Ashby's idea is that the government should introduce a system of employment vouchers, valued at around £3–4,000, for unemployed people unable to find employment after at least two years on ET and a temporary work scheme. The vouchers could be cashed by employers offering them a job contract for a minimum of two years. The scheme could be initiated first in areas of highest long-term unemployment.

19

Rebuilding Initiatives

The Thatcher fiscal revolution – redistributing income to those with most – must be reversed, but in such a way as to extend an incentive-based society to all taxpayers, and particularly those at the bottom of the income pile. While arguments about equity are important in overthrowing the Thatcher tax regime, they are not the only ones. We saw earlier that the move to greater inequality in income had been so marked that it has triggered off a widening of other class differences (detailed in Part I). If class differences are to be narrowed on these fronts, then it is important to establish a greater degree of income equality. This is not a plea for a 'flat earth' policy, with no income differences at all. Clearly there are grounds for income differences, but these should reflect age, experience, skill and responsibility.

Tax Reforms

In what ways, then, can the British income tax system be made more equitable, while at the same time increasing incentives for those at or below average earnings? Here it is important to remember the example cited above (p. 128) of a family man earning £79 net a week, who, because of tax and means-tested benefits, would have to increase his pay by £90 a week in order to achieve an increase in net income of only £17 a week. Tax reform has a crucial part to play in springing the underclass from welfare dependency, as well as building up support for such a programme amongst a much wider group of the electorate.

At the outset, however, it is important to clarify the distinction between marginal and average rates of tax. In public debate, who pays what is invariably presented in marginal tax terms – that is, what a taxpayer will pay on an additional pound in income. However, for most taxpayers there is a marked difference between marginal and average rates of tax, the latter being the amount averaged out for each £1 of income. The reason for this difference is simple. It stems from the structure of income tax, which is built around the idea of tax allowances that can be offset against taxable income. The greater the value of these allowances, the greater the income exempted from tax, and, consequently, the less tax paid to the Exchequer.

This was not always the case. Before the budget of 1920, the British system of direct taxation was based on an exemption principle. Tax allowances were granted, but taxpayers were unable to offset these allowances against their taxable income once their income rose above a specified level. In 1920, Austen Chamberlain transformed the system by allowing tax exemptions to be claimed no matter how big the taxpayer's income. Later, a second change permitted these tax benefits to be offset against income that would otherwise have attracted higher rates of tax.

A system that had been designed to exclude the poor's income from the payment of tax, was reshaped in such a way that, although the poor continued to enjoy exemption on their low income, the same privilege was extended to similar bands of income for all other taxpayers. Because everybody claimed the allowances, the cost of increasing the value of the tax allowances was substantially increased. Add to this cost the growth in government expenditure, and we are a long way in explaining why the real value of the tax threshold, or the level of income at which tax begins to be paid, has fallen during the post-war period. This fall has subjected part of the income of the poor to taxation, while, conversely, continuing to exempt part of the income of well-heeled tax payers.

Apart from personal tax allowances, there is a whole range of other allowances, or benefits, which are gained only on condition that taxpayers undertake a certain pattern of expenditure, such as buying houses, or acquiring a private pension. Despite Mrs Thatcher's rhetoric, bribing people by way of tax allowances is the paternalistic state writ large; taxpayers pick up considerable tax benefits on the condition that they spend their money in ways approved by the Government.

It has been the growth in tax allowances that has allowed the rich to hide behind a smokescreen of high marginal tax rates, while, in reality paying an average rate far below that of many ordinary households (see the answer given to Gordon Brown MP above, in 'Tax Benefits', p. 99). A radical government should commit itself to phasing out these tax allowances. Such a policy must, however, be accompanied by a clear commitment to use the resulting revenue to reduce the rate of tax, as well as to increase child benefit.

The agenda for reform on this issue is made up of a whole range of possibilities. The most modest proposal would be to place a cash limit on all the non-structural tax allowances (that is, on all other than the personal allowances) and to couple this policy to a commitment to use the increase in tax revenue which results to reducing the rate of tax and increasing child benefit. The important role of child benefit in these reforms is discussed below (see also Frank Field, Molly Meacher and Chris Pond, *To Him Who Hath*, Penguin, Harmondsworth, 1977).

This reform would work in the following way. The current expenditure on these tax benefits would be taken as the cash ceiling. The choice of time for instigating the policy would be important here; the cost of mortgage tax relief in 1988 has increased in annual terms from £5 billion to over £6.5 billion. A reduction in interest rates will result in a fall in the size of this subsidy, and the phasing in of a cash ceiling approach ought to be timed to such a favourable point in time. Those organizations whose clients benefit from the subsidy, whether it be the private pensions industry, or the building societies or banks, would be told a year in advance what the cash ceiling was to be, and the organizations would have the task of sharing out the tax subsidy amongst customers, and potential new customers. This would not be an impossible task, given the state of information technology.

An alternative, suggested by Bruce Anderson in the *Sunday Telegraph* (4 September 1988), is to place a time limit on mortgage tax relief. This could, of course, be extended to the whole range of non-personal tax allowances. Anderson's proposal is for the tax subsidy to be limited to a five-year duration. Existing gainers of the subsidy would presumably be given a further five years' grace, and new recruits would similarly benefit. The escalating cost of these tax benefits would be checked within a few years of this policy being implemented.

A more radical proposal is to phase out the allowances over a five-year period, again with the commitment to use the increased revenue coming to the Exchequer to cover cuts in the standard rate of tax and increases in child benefit. With increasing annual incomes, changes in jobs, changes in mortgage interest rates and the like, few people have a static view of what their income and commitments are. It is important, however, to ensure that any move from the present regime to a simplified system should be done at a pace that minimizes the dislocation of people's personal finances.

This latter approach, of phasing out all non-structural tax allowances over the life of a parliament, could become even more radical if the personal allowances were included in the programme. Such a proposal would need to be carefully thought out, and presented to the electorate well before an election campaign. The points that would need stressing are the time-scale over which the reform would be implemented, and the commitment to use the revenue to reduce the standard rate of tax. The phasing out of both personal and non-structural tax allowances would allow a government to reduce the standard rate of tax to between 12p and 15p in the pound. There would also need to be higher rates of tax built on top of this sum.

This root and branch reform of personal taxation has many attractions for those on the left. Because higher-rate taxpayers benefit more from tax allowances than people on lower earnings, the reform would shift the burden of taxation back on to those with highest incomes. Reducing the standard rate of tax to between 12p and 15p in the pound would have an important impact on both the poverty and the unemployment traps. Moreover, such a policy would be seen to be libertarian, in that it genuinely trusted people to spend their own money in ways they prefer, rather than trying to bribe them into centrally determined consumption patterns.

The political advantage of such a reform follows from the timetable for phasing it in. If this proposal was implemented at the beginning of a new parliament, the timetable would allow for increasing tax cuts to be made throughout the parliament, with the largest tax cuts coming just prior to a general election. The reason for this is simple. A cash ceiling approach, or a set timetable to phase allowances out over five years, would result in very little extra revenue in the first year. But from that point onwards, the result of bringing an increasing share of personal income into tax is a commensurate increase in revenue.

Some people on low incomes, however, would be disadvantaged by this reform. Those single people claiming only the single person's allowance, some low-income families with children and part of the pensioner population might find themselves worse off. These tax reforms must therefore be seen as part of the wider reform programme advocated here (see also Frank Field and Paul Omerod, 'The low-tax springboard to freedom', *Guardian*, 2 January 1989). Low income families would be compensated by doubling the value of child benefit over the life of a parliament. Older pensioners, with no occupational pension entitlement, will need to be compensated for the loss of their personal tax allowance (which has the effect of exempting their national insurance pension from tax). Some single people too will need to gain special compensatory measures, although the phasing in of the proposal will do much to minimize any losses.

Doubling the value of child benefit will begin to reshape the welfare state. As we have seen, the major drawback of means-tested assistance – apart from its non-take-up by some groups of the population and the feeling of inferiority that it breeds – is that cash is withdrawn as income rises. The welfare state therefore acts as a ceiling over the heads of those on low incomes, making it difficult for them to move up through their own efforts. In contrast, because child benefit is paid irrespective of income levels, it acts as an income floor on which people can build by their own efforts, and from which there is no disincentive effect. Indeed, the reverse is true. Those without work have the value of their child benefit subtracted from their total welfare payments. The bigger the child benefit, therefore, the bigger the difference between welfare income and income from work for those claimants with children.

How should the increase in child benefit be paid for? While the Government aims to have a nil inflation rate, the prospect of achieving this in the British economy appears slim in the almost indefinite future. One of the results of even a modest rate of inflation is that as people's money income increases, so too does their tax bill. It is suggested that the revenue from fiscal drag, which currently goes in financing the inflation-proofing of personal tax allowances, and which under these proposals would no longer exist, should be used to finance the doubling of child benefit over the life of a parliament. A 1 per cent growth in real incomes results in an additional £0.5 billion surplus accruing to the Exchequer.

Linked to the income tax reforms are two changes to the national insurance contribution system (other reforms affecting entitlement are discussed below). The first reform centres on payments made by employees. The present system operates so that those employees earning less than £43 a week (i.e. the lower earnings limit) make no contribution at all. Above this level, the contribution is graded, with contributions ceasing on incomes above £325 a week. This point is known as the upper earnings limit.

Part III looked at a whole series of forces that locked the underclass into place. One force has been the phenomenal growth in part-time employment. The major reason why Britain now has 40 per cent of all part-time jobs in the EEC is the structure of national insurance contributions which exempt both employers and employees from paying any contributions on earnings of less than £43 a week. However, once the threshold is crossed, *all* income becomes subject to the national insurance tax.

It is necessary to abolish this distorting influence on the labour market. The proposal is for employers' contributions to begin on the first pound of earnings. The aim is for the rates to be adjusted so that, overall, the employer's national insurance contribution does not rise. Given that this reform will hit hardest those firms with most part-time workers, it is suggested that this change is phased in over a five-year period.

This reform, though of crucial importance in countering the current distortion in the job market towards part-time employment, does nothing to help eradicate the high marginal rates of tax faced by people leaving unemployment and gaining work, or of low-paid workers striving to gain real increases in their net take home pay. Even with a 12–15p tax in the pound, a national insurance tax of 9p would almost double the tax rate of most workers, including those on low pay. A second reform is therefore essential – to turn the national insurance tax from a proportional into a progressive tax. A first move is to abolish the national insurance ceiling on contribution. At the current time, workers pay 9 per cent on earnings up to £325 a week. Abolishing this ceiling would generate an additional £1.65 billion per year. The revenue gained from this reform should be used so that contributions rise by single percentage points over bands of income up to the upper earnings limit. Employees' contributions should begin with a 1 per cent contribution from the first £1.00 of earnings. The first band of earnings attracting this contribution should run up to what is now called the lower earnings limit. The aim of imposing this levy is not so much to raise revenue as to bestow contributory rights on lower paid, part-time workers.

Part-time Workers' Rights

Linked to the reforms of the national insurance system are a set of proposals to strengthen the rights of workers who work less than a full week. As was seen in Part III, full-time employment – and to a much lesser extent part-time employment – is the gateway to a whole range of occupational welfare. While for high-income earners this welfare will cover subsidies ranging from the cost of housing, acquiring shares in the company and towards the cost of housing, the most important benefit, both in terms of the numbers of workers covered, and its value, is the occupational pension. Few firms give part-time workers equal rights to such benefits, and many exclude them entirely.

The reforms in national insurance contributions will abolish the in-built bias currently in existence to create part-time employment. Without the incentive to employ workers for whom no national insurance contributions are payable, employers may more rationally decide on whether new job opportunities warrant full- or part-time status. Similarly, because there will be no financial penalty to the employers, more employees will be allowed to determine the length of their own working week. The reform of the national insurance system advocated here will also lead to all workers building up entitlement to national insurance benefits. Currently, 2.7 million part-time workers acquire no national insurance record (*Hansard*, 4 November 1988, col. 813). But a further extension of welfare citizenship is required, and a reform of the pension law is required so that workers are not prevented from entering the scheme on grounds of the numbers of hours worked. While this reform may seem small in itself, it will play an important part in the overall strategy being advocated here of people being able to draw an income from work, wealth, as well as welfare.

20

Spreading Wealth

Moves to overhaul the income tax system must be accompanied by similar changes in wealth taxation. It has been seen how the Thatcher Governments have been busy in turning the taxation of wealth into a voluntary tax. An immediate objective should be the introduction of a wealth tax, which, combined with other taxes, would initiate a substantial redistribution of wealth.

Capital Shares Tax

One of the advantages of being in government is that measures can be initiated that begin to shape public opinion. One such move of an incoming radical government should be to initiate a new Domesday Book, so that the true extent of the vast disparities of wealth is brought home to the voters. The idea would be to compile over a short period a national register of wealth holdings. People would be required to enter their own wealth holdings, and wealth from which they benefit or may benefit, which is held in family trusts. Wealth held abroad would also need to be included. The penalty for not entering an accurate record in the new Domesday Book would be that after the new vesting day for the exercise, all that wealth in Britain not entered in the record would become available for redistribution by the Government. Similarly, those who fail to make accurate returns of their wealth held abroad would be unable to remit back into this country the income from the wealth, so making residence here difficult.

The proposal is not to introduce a wealth tax under the form that it has been proposed elsewhere. Rather, what is being proposed is a capital shares tax. Traditionally, a wealth tax has been considered as another means whereby the Treasury can raise funds. A capital shares tax uses the concept of a wealth tax as a starting point – that is, as a means of raising revenue by a levy on wealth – but goes beyond this by proposing how this revenue could be used. Under this proposal, the resulting revenue would be earmarked (no doubt against strong Treasury opposition) for a fund, from which capital sums could be paid to selected groups in the population. For illustrative purposes, I suggest that two specific groups should be made eligible for these capital grants – those aged twenty, on the threshold of independence, and those at forty-five, the ideal time for career reassessment and a possible fresh start. The aim of a capital shares tax is to enable people starting out on their careers and those wishing to make a mid-career switch to have some 'seed money' to test their entrepreneurial skills.

Two questions need to be addressed. How much money would be available, and how large would the capital grant be paid out from the fund to these eligible groups? In 1967, the TUC published a proposal for a 3 per cent tax on wealth holdings of more than £20,000 a year. This proposal has since been updated, using data from 1986 (see table 20.1). The threshold, which in this illustration is assessed at above £100,000 a year, exempts 97 per cent of the population from the new tax; of course, the threshold would be even higher if assessed according to 1988 data. Moreover this, exercise is intended as an illustration and not as the presentation of a detailed proposal for a

Table 20.1 *Revenue raised from a wealth tax in 1986[a]*

Range of net wealth £	Marginal rate of wealth tax %	Number of cases[b] 000s	Amount of net wealth £m	Revenue £m
0–100,000	0	15,981	448,478	0
100,000–200,000	3	829	105,722	685
200,000–300,000	3	215	45,237	712
Over 300,000	3	159	93,332	2,323
Total		17,184	692,769	3,720

[a] Based on the estimated distribution of the identified wealth of individuals.
[b] Most husbands and wives counted as one tax unit.

Source *Inland Revenue Statistics*, 1988, table 10.3.

capital sharing tax. There is a clear case for grading the tax along progressive lines on wealth holdings in excess of £300,000.

These latest figures carry an air of unreality. For example, less than 3 per cent of the population are listed as holding assets of more than £100,000, which must be a long-passed milestone for most middle-class people living in the south, and an increasing number in the north too.

Using the 1986 figures, a 3 per cent levy on holdings over £100,000 would generate £3.7 billion a year. Setting the threshold at £200,000, which would include all but 1 per cent of taxpayers, would still yield more than £3 billion.

What level of capital sum could be paid out of this fund to the two target groups? Currently about 900,000 people celebrate their twentieth birthday (although this total will fall by a quarter within the next decade), while an average of 600,000 people reach the age of forty-five, a total of 1.5 million people. If the sum raised by a capital sharing tax was around £3.7 billion per annum, this would permit individual capital grants in excess of £2,400. Moreover, the more effective the capital shares tax became, and the more the electorate approves of increases in this tax, the larger any consequent distribution of the derived revenue.

Universal Privatization

Plans to redistribute part of the capital gains resulting from the privatization programme of the Thatcher Governments should also form an integral part of a strategy for sharing wealth. The privatization of industries, ranging from Britoil to British Gas, British Telecom and British Steel, has been a great success, partly because they have touched a public nerve, but also because the share issues have usually been made at below market value. Investors have made considerable capital gains.

Labour's 1987 election policy was to convert the privatized shares into government bonds with a set rate of interest. The advantage of this approach is that it costs nothing, at least in the immediate future. The bonds are merely printed, and the shares confiscated. The obvious disadvantage inherent in such a move would be the adverse reaction among those sectors of the general public who had chosen to invest in such privatized companies. Another disadvantage would be that the interest payable on such bonds would have to be made from public funds. Additionally, if the bonds were sold on the market, they could have an appreciable effect on interest rates and the Government's ability to raise funds in the open market.

An alternative and fairer approach would be for an incoming radical government to insist that each of the privatized industries should make a free issue of stock, by way of compensation for the sale of public assets at deflated prices. This stock could be thinly spread over the entire population, or be given over in its entirety to a number of friendly societies (a new role for the friendly societies is proposed below). These societies would have the duty of distributing the dividends from the shares on either a universal or a restricted basis. This approach could also be linked to reforms that require private sector companies to make over regular, but small parts of the total value of their capital to such a scheme.

There are four major advantages to adopting this approach. It would begin to spread industrial wealth among individuals. It would lessen both the capital value and the size of the dividends gained by those who have made disproportionate gains from privatization. It would begin to make industries accountable to consumers in a way that they patently are not at present; the newly enfranchised shareholders would have the right to participate in elections to the board. It would also begin to ensure individuals a regular, if initially small income that is independent of both work and welfare, which they can spend or save as they please. The exercise of personal initiative also needs to be encouraged on other fronts, and this is the issue that is now considered.

21

Encouraging Initiatives

Three major initiatives are considered here. The first is to allow individuals to act alone in planning their own lives; people should be allowed to capitalize part of the value of their national insurance benefits. The second proposal is to allow people collectively to improve their lot. The illustration here is of offering help to spread credit unions throughout the country. The third looks at a different way of providing collective security, and centres on friendly societies bidding for the social security work the Government intends handing over to agencies, or hospitals opting for trust status within the NHS.

Capitalizing National Insurance Benefits

Different sets of figures are produced on the value of wealth held by different groups of the population. The data show how wealth becomes more evenly spread if occupational, and then state national insurance pension rights are included in the calculations.

There is, of course, a major difference between people who hold most of their wealth in land, or stocks and shares and government bonds, or even gold, compared with those whose 'wealth' is predominantly bound up in their right to an occupational or state pension. Wealth, other than pension entitlements, can be quickly turned into cash or used as security against which to borrow. There is also a difference in the treatment afforded to occupational and state pensioners. Largely because of the tax gains, but also the increased freedom it gives to the pensioner, many pension schemes have provision for allowing part of the value of the pension to be capitalized on retirement. No such scheme exists for state pensioners.

The rules governing national insurance premiums and child benefit should be changed so that people in clearly defined circumstances have the right to capitalize part of the value of these two state benefits. It is not proposed that anyone, taken by a whim, should be able to cash in part of the value of either of these two benefits. A local tribunal would decide on the advisability of such a move in each particular circumstance, and the members' common sense would ensure that applications were considered both prudently and sensitively. The rules on how such a capitalization would affect the level of benefit would be tightly drawn in the sense that if, for example, a person capitalized £1,000 of their state pension, their pension, when paid, would be reduced by the amount of £1,000 worth of contributions. Moreover, if the person found themselves on income support when old, the calculations for income support would assume they were receiving their full old-age pension. There would therefore be no chance of a person claiming part of the value of their benefits, knowing that, at a later stage, he or she could have the difference made up from means-tested assistance. The rules, however, would allow people to repay the capital sum at a later date if they wished to, and were able to do so.

Some people may wish to try their luck in using part of the capital value of their benefits to finance a business venture. Others would use this capitalization to acquire their own house. But this move could be important in increasing a person's employability. Some employers 'black list' recruits living in certain areas. To be able to move to a small terraced house in a more desirable area could result in winning a job when the opportunity arose. Two recent examples from my own constituency – and which prompted me to think of this idea – illustrate the advantage of giving people this freedom.

The first comes from a constituent who works in a local factory and earns £67 a week net for a full week's work. Her son has recently left home, and, at this point she became ineligible for housing benefit. Her unrebated council rent and rates totals £44 a week. But because the council is behind in adjusting people's entitlement to benefit, she continued to draw housing benefit during 1988 on the assumption that her son was still part of her household. She now has a bill of £500 from the council for over-payment of housing benefit, a sum that she has difficulty in repaying on a net income after rent of £23 a week. This constituent has pointed out that, given house prices in Birkenhead, if she can begin buying her own house she could cut her housing costs by over half – to around £20 a week. She would also be acquiring a capital asset. But because of the council's incompetence, which has meant that her rent card is now marked as owing rent, and lacking a deposit, she would be dependent on a somewhat shady mortgage company for the mortgage to buy such a house (rent cards are the easiest and most common means of checking on the credit-worthiness of a person on a low income). Being able to capitalize part of her pension would allow her to present herself at one of the main building societies with a deposit, to halve her housing costs, and begin acquiring a capital asset that would last with her into old age.

The second example is that of a young mother who, while not in a tower-block, lives on the top floor of a maisonette. Under the current housing rules, she has no chance of being rehoused in the near future in a low-rise block in one of the decent areas of Birkenhead, or of gaining a house with a garden. She has three children, one under the age of one, and has to come up four flights of stairs to her home many times a day. She has to carry up the children, her shopping and any other goods coming into the household. This family's life would be transformed if they could buy a small terraced house with a garden. The mother has no savings. Again, if she could trade in a small part of the total value of the child benefit accruing to her, she would have a sizeable sum to present as a down-payment on a house.

Credit Unions

Allowing people to capitalize their national insurance benefits is an example of building ladders from poverty that allow individuals to escape. Credit unions provide similar opportunities, but here the action is organized on a collective basis.

In essence, a credit union, which is a non-profit-making financial co-operative, is formed by a group of people who have a common identity. This common bond can be based on living in the same area, or working in the same factory, or attending the same church, or being members of the same club. Or, it may come from possessing the same ethnic origin. Membership entails the pledging of a weekly sum to be saved, and the agreement that loans will be made from this common pool of savings – at a rate of interest currently fixed by law at no more than 1 per cent. This compares with some loan sharks who can charge in excess of 10,000 per cent! The interest gained from the money is used to cover the operating costs of the union, and any surplus can be put towards a dividend on savings, although the savings return is limited by a ceiling of 8 per cent. In essence, then, credit unions are owned and controlled by their members through elected officials. As members are in fact borrowing from friends, neighbours or colleagues, the extent of default is minimal.

The credit union movement in Great Britain lags far behind that in many other countries. They first appeared in this country in the early 1960s, owing to the impetus in Irish and West Indian communities. The legal framework within which they operate was established by the Credit Union Act of 1979. The activities of the unions are supervised by the Registrar of Friendly Societies. By 1988, there were about ninety unions in existence, with 21,000 members.

This contrasts sharply with other countries. In the United States, for example, there are almost 17,000 unions, with nearly one in five of the population, or 54 million people, as members. In Ireland, credit unions have been in existence for a decade longer than in Britain, but there are now over 450 unions, with a membership exceeding three-quarters of a million. The Irish credit union movement has been strongly supported by the Catholic Church.

The advantages of credit unions are as considerable as they are obvious. Above all, they give people a sense of having a greater control over their own destiny. This is apparent to anyone who sat in on the proceedings of a local credit union. The union also has other, practical advantages. In Ireland, the coverage of unions is now so extensive that the loan sharks have been almost driven out of business. Indeed, with the beginnings of credit unions in this country, one group that has shown considerable interest in this development has been this group of lenders whose business has been with poor people. Giving loans at low rates of interest is only one advantage – although a significant one. The union itself, in consultation with the member, discusses the person's total finances, the reason for the loan and the maximum amount to be borrowed is related to the size of the repayment and to the total income. The union thus helps people develop a greater sense of money management. A further advantage of these unions is that money saved locally is spent locally, rather than being switched to other areas, as often occurs with normal banking arrangements.

Credit unions, while initiating from the wish of people to have greater control over their own affairs, do not come into existence spontaneously. A great deal of planning and preparation is needed. The credit unions in Birkenhead took two years from the decision to start a union to opening the doors for business. There is therefore a need for a number of central bodies that have the resources to enable them to respond to local initiatives, and the staff to see these initiatives through to fruition. A government determined to give poorer people a larger say over their own lives would set aside a small capital sum to support the central finance of credit unions. The aim would be to have covered every area of the country where interest was shown in a union within a ten-year period. There are a few other initiatives that, for a capital sum of a few million pounds, hold the prospect of bringing forward such a radical transformation of the immediate circumstances of poorer people, and the extent to which they control their own lives.

Friendly Societies

The Government is set on a scheme that will result in the biggest social services shake-up since the national insurance scheme was established in 1911. These proposals present both a challenge and an opportunity to radicals. The challenge arises from the fact that the Government is considering turning the day-to-day running of the social security system over to agencies. The idea is that the Government would maintain a central funding role, and would lay down the rates of benefit, while at the same time encouraging organizations, possibly private ones, to handle the payments to customers.

The left has yet to wake up to the new politics as played by the Prime Minister. Demonstrations, resolutions, debates in the Commons are all important in raising morale of those who oppose Mrs Thatcher, and in presenting a continual election campaign to the electorate. They do not, however, have much effect on the Government's programme. It is none the less possible for opponents to pick up the ball, so to speak, when Mrs Thatcher has put it down. The proposed reforms in the delivery of social security benefits to customers is a case in point. They offer the trade unions and other organizations on the left a chance of shaping the post-Thatcher agenda. But if the labour movement is to take advantage of this Thatcher initiative, it first has to rediscover its roots.

A trade union movement anxious to extend rather than limit its influence would seek to regain those functions that the state has stripped from it. Much of the welfare state in this country was built up through voluntary effort, in the vanguard of which were the friendly societies. It was through these benefit or friendly societies that working people began collectively to provide insurance against the loss of income through unemployment, and to ensure that each should have a respectable funeral.

This is not an argument for dismantling or privatizing the welfare state, or for reducing benefit levels. What the Government's proposals offer is not only the chance to seize the initiative from Mrs Thatcher on this front, but to begin to think carefully about what is meant regarding the devolution of power. Responding to Mrs Thatcher's initiative is one way in which radicals build up over time an alternative election programme. Bidding for the proposed agency work allows the left to open up a new debate, and above all begins a dialogue with the voters on what is meant in everyday terms by a devolution of power.

Those seeking a central role for the state will doubtless query the advantages of setting up friendly societies competing for members, when a universal service is provided by the state. But it is partly because the social security system is centrally run, overworked and understaffed that the customers all too often receive such a poor service.

Under any new system, the Government has made plain that it will lay down the minimum rates of benefit. Benefit societies, governed by these minimum conditions, would provide competition clearly lacking under the present system. Those dissatisfied with one friendly society would be able to transfer their entitlements to another. Another way of attracting more customers – apart from providing a better day-to-day service – would be to offer a higher, or different range of benefits on top of the national insurance benefits. These would have to be actuarially based, and increased contributions would be required. Such a strategy would allow benefit societies to begin cutting into the insurance market, which is at present totally dominated by the private pension organizations.

There will, of course, be difficulties with this proposal. The societies would need to initiate recruiting campaigns, and trade union skills and organization would be crucial to their success. But the difficulties seem small in contrast to the success that awaits the left. Above all, responding now to initiatives launched by the Thatcher Government ensures that the alternative programme is not one cobbled together just before a three-week election campaign.

22

Income Floors

These changes aimed at encouraging personal involvement and initiative need to be reinforced by a major overhaul and recasting of the welfare state. Here we are concerned with a form of corporate provision that can also be used to provide at one and the same time a safety net and a reward for initiative. Two reforms are singled out here that will help begin the process of reshaping the welfare state to fulfil both of these objectives.

Incentive-based Welfare

A major reason why so many people live on low incomes is that national insurance benefits, such as old-age pensions and unemployment pay, are paid at below the income support and housing benefit levels. Beveridge was aware that, with few private resources to fall back on, most people would become poor unless basic national insurance benefits were paid at above the level that society deemed to be the minimum income level. Ironically, implementing a programme to raise people above this poverty level may, initially, be far from popular, although sweeteners, like a double Christmas bonus, will do much to pacify any adverse reaction.

The reason for this stems from the relationship between national insurance and income support rates, and the rules about eligibility for the latter. A person may be eligible for income support if their income is below their income support entitlement. Income support is means tested. Any increase in national insurance benefits are offset against the additional benefit that claimants obtain from income support. An increase in the national insurance rates, without a commensurate rise in income support, means that those on income support gain no net increase in benefit. To prevent this happening, increases in pensions and other major benefits are matched by increases in levels of what was, until 1988, supplementary benefit, and has since then been called income support. Such an approach ensures that those who are poor gain the full national insurance benefit increases. But the net effect has been to leave exactly the same number dependent upon means-tested assistance. How can this vicious circle be broken?

A policy of increasing income support rates in line with the annual review of national insurance benefits is the proper one to adopt when national insurance benefits are increased to take account only of changes in inflation since the last review. But should this approach be followed if a future government should decide to make an across-the-board increase in national insurance rates that is significantly above the increase in prices?

This was the 1987 election commitment by the Labour Party. This proposal is discussed here as a way of illustrating the main principles involved in lessening dependence on means tests, while at the same time extending the idea of social citizenship which stems from the national insurance system.

The Labour Party's commitment was to raise pensions by £5 for a single person and £8 for a married couple. The reason for this pledge was to make good the cut in benefits that resulted from the breaking of the link between these benefits and earnings or prices – whichever most favoured the claimant. The academic point that the proposed increase did not, in fact, make good the shortfall that beneficiaries suffered is left to one side.

How many pensioners would be floated off means-tested income support if a £5 and £8 increase in the national insurance pension was not matched by a similar change in the income support rates? The House of Commons Library has made some calculations based on the December 1984 Supplementary Benefit Annual Statistical Inquiry. At that time, there were 1.4 million pensioners receiving supplementary benefits of less than £5 a week. Had the national insurance pensions been increased by an additional £5 a week over and above the inflation rate, and supplementary benefit uprated by the rate of inflation only, then virtually all of the 1.4 million claimants would no longer be entitled to supplementary benefit. Similarly, other pensioner households, containing married couples, would be floated off supplementary benefit by an increase in the married couple's rate of £8 a week. The

cost of increasing retirement pensions by this amount was estimated at
£1.65 billion. Such a move would have greatly simplified the supplementary benefit system, as fewer people eligible for benefit would
have been on the books of local social security offices. However, many
of the 1.3 million recipients who would have ceased to be eligible for
supplementary benefit were receiving what is called certificated housing benefit.

The Government points out that, for example, although this group
would have lost entitlement to supplementary assistance, 1.2 million of
them would have gained entitlement to standard housing benefit. In
other words, they would still be dependent on a means-tested housing
benefit in order to ensure that their income was paid at the minimum
level laid down by Parliament. The Minister of State for Social
Security, in outlining his calculations, demonstrated that increases of
£5 and £8 in the pensions would have lead to only 100,000 ceasing
entirely to draw means-tested assistance (letter from John Major, MP,
to the author, 7 October 1986). But these data do not give an accurate
account of the overall effect of their change, for an additional 380,000
standard housing benefit recipients would have had an income above
their entitlement level. In other words, there would be an overall
decline of nearly half a million people (that is, 380,000 + 100,000)
drawing means-tested support.

A further 'simplification' of the system would occur if a substantial
and real increase was made in child benefit. Let us assume that the
value of child benefit, currently at £7.25, be doubled (as is proposed as
part of the tax changes in chapter 19). Calculations, again by the
House of Commons Library, suggest that such an increase would lead
to a reduction of families drawing means-tested supplementary benefit, and family credit.

None of these calculations, however, can take account of changes in
the climate in which people operate, and the resulting change in
attitudes and behaviour. With the increasing dominance of a means-
tested assistance, people have not only become passively dependent as
the Government claims. The position is far worse. A new lifestyle has
developed, whereby the energy of many people on means-tested
assistance is channelled into what is called 'working the system'. As
there are few opportunities for making it by oneself, a great deal of the
effort of those in low-income groups goes into working out how they
can maximize their income within the existing rules.

A move such as raising the real value of national insurance benefits, and of child benefit in particular, will, I believe, begin to change the psychological attitude of claimants, by allowing the extraordinary effort and intelligence that is currently absorbed into 'working the system' to be channelled into transforming the status of many currently caught in means-tested assistance.

The changes in child benefit advocated here illustrate the nature of the change that will occur. Child benefit is deducted from other social security entitlements, but is kept in full by parents in work. It therefore acts as a springboard to freedom. For families with two or three children, the doubling of child benefit would mean an increase in their tax-free income from £14.50 to £29 and from £21.75 to £43.50, respectively. I would suggest that this level of support given by child benefit would price many jobs into a claimant's reckoning. It would, in particular, transform the position of many single mothers on income support. Work could become a real possibility for the first time. Such an outcome would be diametrically opposite to Mrs Thatcher's policy of decreasing wages and then penalizing those unemployed people who do not take these very low-paid jobs. The child benefit proposals are also appropriate to the significant changes occurring in the labour market with an increasing number of jobs offered on a less than full-time basis.

Unemployment has played a crucial role both in bringing the underclass into existence and to locking it in place. Measures to reduce unemployment are of the utmost importance and have been outlined above. At the same time, the benefits to the unemployed also need to be considered. In 1957, of the 234,000 unemployed claimants drawing benefit, the majority (153,000) drew unemployment benefit only, while a further 46,000 (or 30 per cent) found themselves totally dependent on means-tested assistance. In 1988, with over 2.5 million unemployed claimants, 504,142 drew unemployment only, while 1.3 million were totally dependent upon income support and a further 131,000 drew both unemployment benefit and income support.

Because flat-rate unemployment benefit can only be drawn for a maximum of a year, a large number of today's unemployed find themselves having to draw means-tested assistance. This rule needs to be changed, so as to allow the unemployed to draw benefit as long as unemployment lasts, providing that claimants have not refused jobs they were offered without good cause, and are prepared to go on training schemes. The charge against such a move is that it will pay unemployment benefit to claimants, some of whose household income already prevents them from being poor. There is some force to this argument, if the only concern is about paying benefits to people in need. Even so, the number of households for which this is true is remarkably small.

All of the official figures show that unemployed claimants invariably have unemployed wives, and the proportion of wives unemployed increases with the length of their husband's unemployment. One reason put forward for this is that a person is more likely to lose their job in an area of high unemployment, and this lack of job opportunities must apply equally to wives. An alternative view, and one that is supported by circumstantial evidence from my own constituency, is that many wives voluntarily cease to work once their husbands become long-term unemployed. The reason for this is that, while their husbands were drawing national insurance unemployment benefit, additional income to the household is not taken into account when determining eligibility for that benefit. Once unemployment benefit ceases, a claimant may become eligible for income support, but such eligibility is affected by his partner's earnings. Apart from a disregard of £5, a partner's earnings are deducted pound for pound from a claimant's income support entitlement. The present rules do not make it worthwhile for most wives to continue working once their husbands join the ranks of the long-term unemployed. A continuation of unemployment benefit for as long as unemployment lasts will ensure that the working wives of men who are unemployed are not penalized. Moreover, working wives provide the family with a contact to the world of work where news about job opportunities is first picked up. Keeping wives in work will therefore maximize the chances of their husbands hearing about possible job openings.

Single-parent Families

The increase in the number of single-parent families has been detailed in Part I. The rise has been so significant that, had it not been overshadowed by the advent of mass unemployment, much of today's public debate about welfare reform would be centred on how best to help this group of claimants. While some single-parent families have an adequate income, others are poor, and some are destined to remain on welfare for very long periods. Three reforms are proposed. The first is to change what is called the earnings disregard. Under the supplementary benefit system, single parents could earn additional income and only part of this was offset against their benefit. A taper was applied over a sliding scale of income, but on average the formula worked out so that most single parents would be able to earn an additional £12 without losing benefit entitlement. More importantly, they were able to offset totally any child-minding costs they incurred while going out to work.

One of the Government's aims in moving from supplementary benefit to income support was to simplify the system. This has been achieved, but at the cost of stifling personal initiative. Instead of a sliding scale to determine what income a single parent in work can keep without losing benefit, a standard £15 cut-off point has been introduced. While this sum is just above the average sum of additional income earned by single parents under the previous system, the new rules, again in the name of simplification, have abolished the claimants right to offset child-minding costs against their earnings. The consequence is that most single parents, who have to pay someone to look after their children while at work, are now worse off if they continue part-time work, and the number of single parents in work is likely to drop dramatically because of this change. Given that it is good for many people to get out of the home and meet other people at work, and that it is crucially important not to leave re-entry into the labour market until the person's children have grown up, these disregard rules need to be reversed as soon as possible.

A second reform concerns the payment, or non-payment, of maintainance. At the current time over 1,000,000 men pay no contribution whatsoever towards the cost of raising their children. Again, this position needs to be changed. Being responsible for the birth of a child is one of the most important events in which a human being can be involved. Passing the bill over to the welfare authorities, and thereby to other taxpayers, is not acceptable, either in terms of the escalating size of the bill, or, more importantly, from the point of view of individuals learning about how to behave responsibly, and the long-term financial responsibilities that flow from adult behaviour. Of the 232,255 single mothers receiving supplementary benefit in 1987, only 17,084 had maintainance orders against the father of their children (*Hansard*, 7 November 1988, col. 94).

In 1958, the system of attachment of earnings was instituted in respect of maintenance orders. The scheme was extended in 1967 to fines with the intention of keeping defaulters out of prison. At the current time, all sorts of bodies and organizations can apply to have an attachment of earnings made on someone who owes money. The proposal here is that the right to gain an attachment of earnings should now be limited to maintainance payments only. Two allied reforms are also advocated. The first is that after an initial period single parents should be required to name the father of their children when signing on for welfare. It will then be the responsibility of the Department of Social Security to take out a maintainance order against the father, although the form of the order should be such that the order continues to operate when the mother leaves welfare. Indeed, a crucial part of the new contract between the state and single parents will be for the state to continue paying the mother (and in a few cases the father) the maintenance payments for as long as that person is responsible for a child. It will be the state's duty to recoup these payments from the father. The second reform is that, in order to emphasize the importance of the responsibilities fathers have towards the maintainance of their children, maintainance payments, on a much reduced scale, should continue for people when they are out of work and on welfare themselves.

The last reform on this front centres on the school curriculum. It is becoming more, not less important to provide adequate teaching in schools on personal relationships and on how people should treat one another that goes far beyond straightforward lessons on sex education – important though this is. It is also crucial that vulnerable young girls understand clearly that having a child at sixteen does not usually result in getting a passport to new-found freedom. While claiming £40 a week on welfare may seem a lot to a fifteen-year-old schoolgirl, it is precious little when that is the sum each week on which a family budget has to be maintained. Moreover, the thought of having one's own flat takes on a different vision when it is situated on a sink council estate. Young single parents who have themselves learned by bitter experience what a limitation young parenthood can often be should be used imaginatively in schools to get this message across. It is important to remember that such a campaign would be conducted against the background of the economy moving back to full employment, and therefore of an increasing range of job opportunities for school-leavers. The reforms should similarly be related to those advocated below on lowering the school leaving age to fourteen for those students who have been failed by our present educational system to allow them to undertake part-time work and part-time training.

To increase eligibility for unemployment benefit for the duration of unemployment will cost £600 million, net of savings in income support (*Hansard*, 28 October 1988, col. 458). This move alone will not ensure that the working partner of an unemployed person is not penalized for working. A further objective is to make sure that people do not move out of unemployment to an even lower income from work. The moves to increase child benefit, which have already been discussed, will ensure that most households with children are not faced with this option. The net cost of this reform is £1.6 bn. While the cost of making the changes to the welfare payments to single parents will result in a net saving in public expenditure, this is not the main aim. The overall aim is to ensure that the welfare state encourages rather than penalizes personal initiative. It is also necessary, however, to ensure that the labour market pays adequate rewards, but this policy must be linked to real increases in productivity. We now turn to consider this topic.

Earnings

The Thatcher Governments have been successful in pushing down the relative pay of low-paid workers. This has been brought about by the increase in unemployment and the abolition of the statutory minimum wage, together with a programme of Government ministers exhaulting employers to reduce wage settlements, particularly for the low-paid. In addition, the whole climate of opinion created by the Government has induced some employers to short-change their staff as and when the possibility has arisen.

The move back to full employment, an integral part of the reform being advocated here, will itself have an indirect effect on wage levels, particularly for those at the bottom end of the income pile, although it cannot be stressed enough that the drive towards full employment must be matched by a commitment to improve the productivity of all workers – including those on low pay. But other actions similarly need to be initiated. There is a need to introduce a statutory minimum wage.

There are a number of arguments against such a strategy, and these need to be taken seriously, and, where appropriate, countered in the manner by which the minimum wage is introduced. It is pointed out, for example, that what is of most interest is not pay levels but living standards, and the latter can be more easily influenced through tax and benefit policies. There is some merit in this argument, although the record shows that there is a distinct difference between rhetoric and performance on this issue. Many people who call for benefit increases in a discussion on whether or not to operate a minimum wage, mysteriously lose their voice in debates to enhance welfare payments (Sam Brittan and Joe Rogaly, both from the *Financial Times* stable, are honorable exceptions to this rule). Moreover, this welfare-only approach ignores the opinions of low-paid workers themselves. In a market-orientated society, where every good or service has its price, the low-pay 'price tag' attached to some workers sums up in their eyes the low value placed on them by society. Higher pay is not, therefore, only about an increase in living standards, although this is crucially important, but in gaining respect and an idea of one's worth from the rest of the community. Tax and welfare policies are important, and proposals on these two fronts have already been outlined, but these should supplement an initiative on pay, rather than be a substitute for it.

Currently, the most frequent demand is for a minimum wage level of two-thirds of average earnings to be either implemented immediately, or over a short period. It is worth considering from where this demand came. Back in the mid-1970s, Philip Rowntree gave me the funds to establish the Low Pay Unit (LPU) to campaign on behalf of workers in Wage Council industries.

One of the principle aims of the LPU was to ensure that Wages Councils met at least once a year (many had not done so, despite the rate of inflation at the time). A further objection was to ensure that the independent members received an outside briefing, setting out the case for a substantial increase in pay for the workers covered by that particular Council. It was seen above that while these workers constitute only 14 per cent of the working population, 70 per cent of Wage Council workers can be defined as 'low-paid'. The LPU entered this process as it believed a trade union would. A bargaining position was established that would draw attention to the needs of the lowest paid workers, and, hopefully, lead to a reasonable wage settlement. The target of two-thirds of average earnings was literally pulled out of the air, in order to show how low the pay rates were in Wage Council industries. Its aim was to act as a bluff in the wage negotiations in order to shame the Councils, first into meeting each year, and then setting a respectable wage increase. This, then, was the background to the two-thirds average earnings target.

This level of pay was never conceived of as being a realizable objective for a statutory minimum wage that would be brought in over a short period of time. Given present wage levels, investment and productivity levels, the current demand by some of the left for the implementation of such a target over three years would result in a substantial increase in unemployment (see Frank Field, *The Minimum Wage: Its Prospects and Dangers*, Heinemann, London, 1984).

What is proposed here is a more modest target of 55 per cent of average earnings of all workers, both male and female rates combined in that industry. The target wage for each industry would be implemented over a five-year period, but should be accompanied by a tailor-made programme on training, investment and productivity targets. When these targets had been achieved, with increased skill and investment levels showing up in higher productivity, the proposal would be to implement a higher national minimum wage for all workers, aiming for 60 per cent of average earnings over the following five years. Nothing in this plan would prevent trade unions negotiating higher rates of pay than these target levels.

One major national requirement – also commented on in this concluding section – is to raise the skill levels of British workers. Such an approach is crucial to any successful policy of implementing a minimum wage in low-pay sectors, if the aim is both to raise pay and protect employment. Although again it is important to consider this question on an industry-by-industry basis. In some low-paid industries, and here agriculture is a notorious example, the low pay of workers is accompanied by very high productivity levels. In many other sectors of low pay, however, the level of pay is reflected in low productivity. Indeed, a National Economic Development Office report showed that low pay itself was a probable cause of inefficiency; given the cheapness of labour, it did not pay employers to organize their own side more effectively.

Alongside a programme of raising skill levels is the need to dovetail an investment programme. Indeed, in many industries there would be little point in raising the skill level unless workers are given more advanced capital equipment on which to work. The raising of skills to match rising investment will lead to increased productivity. This itself may lead to fewer people being employed, unless the programme can be accompanied by industries gaining an increased market share of both home and export markets. From this brief description, it can be seen that a policy to deal with low pay has to be seen as a policy in miniature of planning a continuing renaissance of British industry.

Low pay is not only prevalent in some sectors of manufacturing industry. It is also a characteristic of much of the service sector, and also of the public sector. Policies to continue the improvement of productivity in both sectors are crucial. But there will come a point where productivity gains alone will not cover the necessary wage increases. At this point, we the consumers have to be presented with a moral choice. We can continue to gain services at a price that leads to the exploitation of some fellow citizens, whether they work in the private sector, such as in hotels, or in the public sector, as in the health services. Alternatively, we can make the decision that decent wages should be paid to all workers who carry out their duties properly and effectively, and that this increased wage level may need to be reflected in the price of the good or service. To act on the public sector will mean that part of the bill (that is, that part not paid for by improved productivity) will be presented to us as taxpayers.

Of course, consumers as individuals can rarely make such choices operative, even if they wished to. The only way consumers are given an effective option is for politicians to propose policies to achieve such an objective, and to seek support for their endorsement. A policy of raising the wages of the lowest paid, first on an industry basis, and then over the whole country, for this approach to be part of an overall investment and training programme, and for the whole strategy to appear as part of an election manifesto, would provide consumers with the chance of turning a moral decision into an economic reality.

Increasing Skills

Schools fail a significant minority of children. Large numbers leave school without being able to read or write properly, as many employers will testify, and as I am regularly reminded when younger people come to my constituency surgery and are unable to write out their names and addresses. Other young people vote with their feet and leave early by failing to turn up during their last year, and sometimes their last two years at school. Those children who do stay in school, but who feel they are failing, invariably have a disruptive influence. This disgruntled minority has a disturbing impact on the performance of other pupils.

Two major educational reforms are proposed. We saw earlier how children from poorer backgrounds were disadvantaged by their home environment before they reached school, and that a lower proportion of poorer children gained a place at a nursery or a playgroup than did children from richer homes. To counter both the unfavourable home environment, and the difficulty poorer parents have in equalling the sharp elbows of the middle classes, who are well accustomed to taking themselves to the front of the queue, the school starting age for nursery education should be reduced to three. The programme would need to be implemented over time, and the money should first be targeted to those areas with high instances of deprivation. The policy would then need to be made uniform throughout the whole country.

A second reform is to make the school leaving age flexible over the fourteen to sixteen year age band. Disgruntled young people who currently gain nothing positive from their last years at school should be allowed to opt for part-time work at the age of fourteen if they so wish. The new arrangement would be conditional on fulfilling the following conditions. First, the young person would have had to have found a job, and that job would itself have to offer day release, which at the age of fourteen would amount to two days a week. The total time in work could be raised to four days for someone aged between fifteen and sixteen. The day release time could be spent at school or college and the course would be linked to the gaining of technical qualifications. Second, on their sixteenth birthday young people would be required to report for interviews with their youth employment officers. At this stage, they would have to discuss how they wished to employ their right to three years in further education. The aim of both the part-time education and further extended full-time study, on grants, would be to acquire qualifications on a module basis, so as to build up a whole range of technical qualifications. It would therefore be possible for a young school-leaver to begin acquiring qualifications that could lead in the end to gaining a technical degree qualification.

The advantages of such a move are considerable. Many of those who feel they are achieving least, and are most disruptive in schools, would opt for early leaving. Schools would become safer and quieter places, and parents would know that from fourteen onwards the remaining pupils would be specializing for their GCSE and A-level examinations. Opting out into private education, or moving into the catchment area with the best state schools, would become a less important past-time. The policy itself would largely make redundant the politics of selection versus comprehensive education; most of those staying in full-time education in school would be motivated by academic success.

The aim is that those young people who opt for early leaving would themselves be substantial gainers. I have found it impossible to convince young people in the latter stages of their compulsory education of the need to gain skills with which to enter full-time work. The lure of a weekly wage-packet has a mesmerizing effect. Under the scheme proposed here, young people would gain the wage-packet, would not lose contact with education (they would be in college or school, initially for two days a week) and would have gained an employer interested in developing their skills. Once these young people became achievers, both in keeping down a job for part of the week, and by acquiring skills relevant to the work, their self-esteem would be enhanced. Once these young people begin to see that they, too, can be achievers, a mini-revolution will have been accomplished.

One positive result of a newly motivated group would be that some might see the advantages to themselves of returning to full-time education at the age of sixteen. They would be coming back to education, however, to build upon the qualifications they had already begun to acquire, and would feel at least equal, if not superior in some respects, to their peers who had remained in full-time education. Again, the aim would be for employers to back this decision with the offer of future employment once the education or training course had been completed.

One objection that is bound to be raised by those who are conditioned to defending the status quo is to point to the current labour market and the difficulties being experienced by young people attempting to find work. Everything in chapter 11 points to the validity of this argument.

It is important, however, to distinguish between the current situation and what the future holds. Already, the job market is changing. Some companies are so short of staff that they are offering their women workers flexible hours, together with substantial sums to cover their child-minding costs. Similarly, some of the bigger employers are finding it impossible to attract young workers on to their YTS schemes. In an attempt to maintain their share of the young labour market, employers are finding it necessary to offer their own training courses, on the rates of pay currently going to young people in the labour market, rather than the YTS trainee pay level.

Future projections show a marked fall in the numbers of young people entering the labour market. It is estimated that the number of people aged between sixteen and nineteen will fall by over 850,000 between 1987 and 1995 – a reduction of nearly 25 per cent. (*Labour*

Market Quarterly Report, Training Commission, July 1988, p. 11.) Indeed, the fall is so dramatic that for the NHS to maintain current nursing levels will require it cornering half of all available female school-leavers with good O-level results (five higher grade O levels, or one A level). Similarly, fewer than twenty large employers currently account for the employment of over half the estimated 27,000 leavers with A-level equivalent qualifications (for details see *Labour Market Quarterly Report*, published by the Training Commission, July 1988, pp. 11–12). There could hardly be a more opportune time for attempting to salvage something for those young people who are currently gaining little if anything from the educational system.

While this reform is specifically designed to prevent many of today's disgruntled education consumers joining the ranks of tomorrow's underclass, it will of course have implications for a much wider group of young people, whose talents and needs have been all too little met by the emphasis on the reorganization of secondary education to the exclusion of all other considerations. The proposal of a flexible school leaving age is aimed to buy time while considering the major changes that should take place in secondary education. An official enquiry is needed to examine why the skills acquired by some children in primary schools are *lost* during their time in a secondary school. But this policy of buying time should not be at the expense of those young people who are currently losing out at school. Hence this proposal to combine the world of work and education in a package which might prove attractive to people who are otherwise likely to be recruited into the underclass.

CONCLUSION

A number of significant changes have occurred in British society since 1979, and the one centred on in this book has been the emergence of an underclass. Throughout modern times, there has existed in Britain a large number of people who were poor – although, for various reasons, the numbers have sometimes been exaggerated. *Losing Out* has argued that, since 1979, a minority of the population has been progressively cut off from other people on low income, let alone those on average or high incomes. A number of factors have contributed to this state of affairs. One significant cause has been a redistribution of income towards richer people on a scale without parallel this century. This redistribution of income, backed up by a similar strategy on wealth, has resulted in a widening of class differences for the first time since 1945. Unemployment has also played a part as a recruiting sergeant for the underclass, both in the way it has selected its membership, and in the way it has held them in place. Unemployment is also a significant cause of downward mobility in Britain. The redistribution of income and wealth has been matched by a realignment of people's political allegiances with an increasing number of those with modest resources allying themselves with the most prosperous sections of the community. The underclass has therefore become separated, both in terms of income, life chances and political aspirations.

Separation has also occurred on somewhat more nebulous but equally important grounds. A feeling of belonging to a community, or as it has been described here, of citizenship, is built up from a whole range of social, economic and psychological components. Psychologically, the underclass is being increasingly isolated by the growth of a drawbridge mentality amongst those who feel they are 'making it' in Thatcher's Britain. Economically, the underclass has become separated by a rebuttal from the labour market, combined with a Government policy to prevent the products of economic growth being shared amongst all sections of the community. Accompanying the exclusion from the labour market has been a policy of disenfranchising the underclass from full welfare citizenship. This disenfranchising policy will be taken a stage further in the political domain, with the linking for the first time for fifty years of the right to vote with the payment of contributions to local government exchequers.

This section has been concerned with outlining policies aimed at freeing the underclass from the political, economic and social apartheid into which they are being pushed. But to implement these policies requires winning political power, and therefore the debate about the future of the underclass is itself part of the debate about the future of left politics in Britain. There is little point devising programmes that will appeal only to Britain's newly dispossessed. Rather, the appeal has been one that is also relevant to wide sections of the electorate. It is an appeal that combines self-interest with altruism. It is a programme that holds out more than hope for the underclass. But to deliver this programme successfully will require an invigoration of left politics, where hope for the dispossessed spreads to a sure-founded belief amongst the electorate that there is, after all, a worthwhile life after Thatcherism.

Index

197